H. A. Reuschlein.

July 3, 1950.

THOMAS DE QUINCEY
CONFESSIONS OF AN ENGLISH
OPIUM-EATER

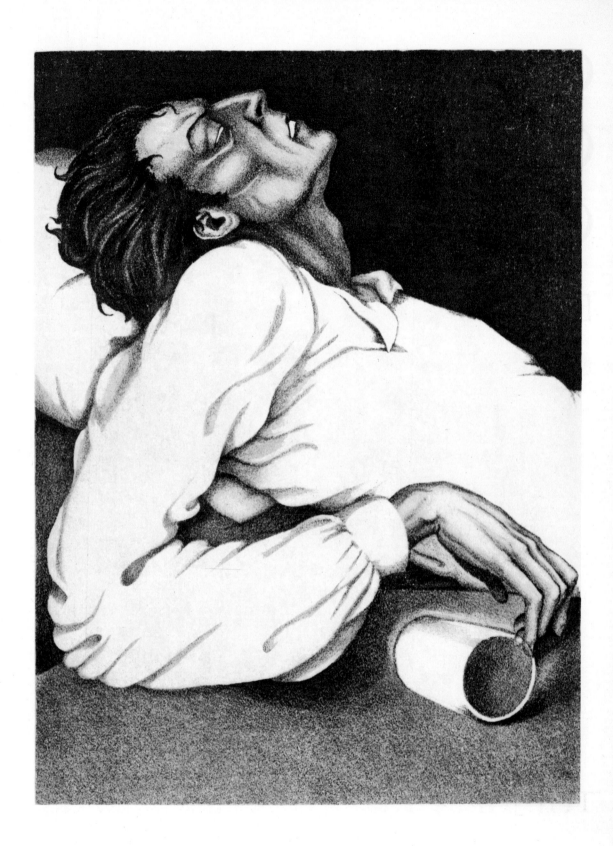

CONFESSIONS OF AN ENGLISH OPIUM-EATER

BY THOMAS DE QUINCEY

With an Introduction by William Bolitho

and Twelve Gravures by Zhenya Gay

THE HERITAGE PRESS, NEW YORK

CONTENTS

The Gravures by ZHENYA GAY *are placed to face the following pages:*
2, 10, 18, 22, 30, 38, 46, 54, 62, 66, 74.

INTRODUCTION

THE AUTHOR of this book, which is one of the best books of the world, was born in Greenheys, near Manchester, in the year 1785, on the 15th of August. It is legitimate to enquire after and to supply this sort of trifling detail about the life of a genius, on express condition—under pain, that is, of misunderstanding life, literature and art—of taking them for only what they are. That is, appendages, more or less superfluous, and at any rate un-essential to the biography itself. Thomas de Quincey's autobiography is this book. If you notice that it ends abruptly, that it is extremely selective of events and dates, and last of all that it deals only with his youth, you are near to stumbling upon the inner laws of biography as a valid art. For whatever the extent of the miscomprehension which has produced volumes of anecdotes, dossiers of careers, analytical studies of fates, that alone fully deserves the title of a biography which deals, as de Quincey here dealt, with the person as such. The piece is here complete. What after and before happened to him is annex. In his case all was completed by his eighteenth year, and it was his own theory that such is a general law for humanity; that the man himself is his youth and not his age.* Here is the portrait. The rest is wear and tear on it.

So here is another instance for the good, established practice of reading the preface last, the crumbs after the banquet. His father was a gentleman and a merchant, in the trade with Lisbon and the West Indies, with a small library and a comfortable fortune. He died in his thirty-ninth year, of consumption, leaving his large family modestly provided for.

His mother's maiden name was Penson. She was the daughter of an officer in the army, a sensible woman who could write a good letter. The family therefore was intellectually, like their fortunes, of the good middle sort, or somewhat above. You have learnt from the book itself of its claims to antiquity and of its cousin-ship with the American Quincys—a nation for which, like many of his friends and contemporaries, such men as Shelley, Coleridge, Blake, he had and expressed always only respect and admiration. That was the way of those great times, which lesser Englishmen disused. He seemed always almost as proud of the transatlan-tic fruiting of his family as of his Norman descent, which is guaranteed by the Chronicle of Robert of Gloucester.

* "Youth, however eclipsed for a season, is un-doubtedly the proper, permanent, and genuine condition of man; and if we look closely into this dreary delusion of growing old . . ."
—Nathaniel Hawthorne.

i

He was the fifth child and the second son of the marriage. Two particulars of his childhood, recalled by himself in another essay, may be worth keeping in mind. The first was his early propensity to dreams and reveries, which, as he noticed, is a proof that his later prodigious power in this "night-art" was not due to, if improved by, his laudanum. The second, which is extremely mysterious and touching, is that at the age of three he, as it were, rehearsed, in the death of his little sister Jane, the tragedy of the loss of Ann. It appears that a few days before the child's death there was some whispering among the other servants and children, which he overheard, of cruelty done to her by the nurse. He said, of its effect on him: "I did not often see the person charged with this cruelty, but when I did, my eyes sought the ground. The feeling which fell upon me was a shuddering horror, as upon a first glimpse of the truth that I was in a world of evil. I knew little more of mortality than that Jane had disappeared."

The space between this infancy and the first days of the Confessions is small. I will only insert into it that he, like most of the rest of his family, seemed consumptive; and that early death from that disease was mournfully common in their annals. The leader of his boyhood was his brother William, a strong and daring boy, in whose train, unwillingly, he marched against the urchins of the factory workers of the vicinity. For already the "dark Satanic mills" had begun to blacken the air of young Manchester, and the gigantic tragedy of the birth of the modern proletariat had commenced. This was the same strange and attractive William who at ten years old, from brooding on ghost stories, conceived the speculation, which his brother Thomas himself would not have disowned, of the danger to the human race of a confederation of all ghosts and spectres against the living. William died at sixteen of the typhus fever.

The school years, the tangled quarrels with his guardians, his growth as a scholar, the reasons for his flight and fall into the power of London, already the largest city in the world, is set forward in his own narrative, and needs neither repetition nor enlargement. The inquisitive may be told that the name of the guardian, whose temporary domestic happiness and sad fate he gives such a touching picture of in the Confessions, was Kelsall, who succeeded to the de Quincey business in Manchester. So in this Kelsall's downfall was involved, spiritually, the extinction of the hopes and practical life of de Quincey's father.

And now, briefly, to summarize what happened afterwards to the young man of the Confessions. He never found Ann. By a ruinous arrangement with the money-lenders, he finally managed to get to College: Worcester College, Oxford. London memories went up with him: "Those profound revelations which had been ploughed so deeply into the heart, those *encaustic* records which in the

ii

mighty furnaces of London life had been burned into the undying memory by the fierce action of misery." In this temperament it is not surprising that, where many of the most magnificent dunces of England succeeded, were confirmed even, and consecrated, de Quincey failed. He left without taking his degree.

It was before this, in his second year at college, that he began the use of that prodigious opium, the great *pharmakon nepenthes*. It was at the instance of a fellow collegian, and no doubt under the influence of the example of Coleridge, whose habit was then the talk and wonder of England. The occasion, and his reflections on it, is in the head of the book.

And now the register of his life, as I forewarned you, is to me, at any rate, rather anticlinal to where you left him. He became acquainted with Wordsworth and Coleridge and the host of menial spirits that encumbered them; and took up residence in a cottage in the Lake Country. This he exchanged at various times for lodgings in London and Edinburgh. His dealings with his set have naturally two phases. He was their faintly, and most unjustly patronized, friend. And to most of them he lent money to his ruin. He married, had children, and earned his living by writing that incomparable mass of essays for the reviews and newspapers; of which the most exciting (to be rash) is the marvel of imaginary or perhaps only imaginative history, *The Flight of the Kalmuck Tartars*; the wittiest and strangest, *Murder Considered as One of the Fine Arts*. But in its unexampled profusion, value and interest, this corpus is not to be spoken about hurriedly, but rather as the *Chasidim* prepare for writing the sacred name, only after fitting a new pen, and washing the hands.

It is perhaps because of some stupid misapprehension, induced by the form of this vast life-work, put out as it was "journalistically" and not volume by volume, that is due a certain underestimation of his place in literature, both that which I told you there was suspicion of among his friends themselves, and one in the general opinion of his times, which is the historical, though not logical basis of that which prevailed among the English critics of yesterday. There is a certain snobbishness in the literary matter; even cultivated people have a strain of sheep-blood in their veins, which makes them love the old detours. The same dull persons who abolished Keats and said Blake was an amiable lunatic underestimated this genius. To him they reproached the discursiveness of its subject matter, the form of its invariable publication—the *Confessions* themselves were first printed by instalments in *The London Magazine*, and the legendary charge that he could never finish anything. The truth in the last is that the *Confessions* are no more finished than *The Tempest*, just as *King Lear* has no beginning; for as old John Lyly said deeply, "In art there's no perfection." To be sure, no

iii

modern advocate of the devil in the interminable de Quincey case would put these charges—or he would bite his tongue the moment after. De Quincey is kept out of his place, on the same dais as Sir Thomas Browne, Jeremy Taylor, Donne, of the greatest prose-writers of English literature (which, believe me, carries the same rank as world literature), by a new set of "diminishments" brought up by the partisans of the feminine prose in the '90's, who hold still a sort of *fainéant* authority to-day. He is too rhetorical for them, like Browne and Milton, whose prose has yet escaped indictment on the same charge. Prose, they say, should walk, and not fly; no, more, it should knit, and embroider, and fetch water, and do all the tasks Hercules himself under the same tyranny of women and eunuchs was forced to submit to. And so once too, for the whole length of another century, Shakespeare was put beneath Colley Cibber. But I have no brief, nothing but the noble duty of celebration of a great man's masterpiece. In this I may indifferently start, either with its literary or its philosophical quality.

This book, as I wrote, sets out the picture of a soul, a psycho-graph; and as such it outranks all such that our marvellous literature possesses: *Lavengro*, and *Father and Sons*, *Mark Rutherford*, and *The Way of All Flesh* . . . let me be excused from any ragged enunciation of the mere names of such treasures. The subject is in the first place of quality. More interesting, difficult and moving specifications could not perhaps be found than those which it possesses. For here is the portrait of a scholar, a young scholar (at the height of the book he is perhaps seventeen) who is poor even to chronic starvation, a lover of a certain very delicate sort, and, which never does any harm, a gentleman of breeding. I would divide the story of his spiritual adventure into three parts. There is his relation to the old City; to the girl, the waif Ann, and then his terrific flight into the world of dreams. Underneath all these, as the abysmal mud underlies the deep sea, is the working of that "mighty phantom," opium; strictly unnecessary, I might surmise, to the workings of these themes, but like the last bass of an organ, a most powerful and luxurious accompaniment.

So it is not only the portrait of de Quincey but of London, and by surcrease of all great old cities. What an inspiration of life, to set this boy in her murkiest, most mysterious shadow, city life, like a bright candle! In a fat sleek countryside, he would have given us books, and no one can do more than guess what they might have been. But who then could have worked like him in the impalpable melancholy of all places where man has lived and died in, in millions for generations, the soul of street lamps, and street shadows? Scenery which because it is stained through with humanity's passing generations has greater depths and heights than any abstract Alps of nature. Do you read again that exalted two

iv

pages in which, beginning with his relation of his habit of hearing music at the
Italian Opera, in his periodical "debauches of opium," he wanders through the
labyrinthine streets, seeing the common people at their Saturday night's market-
ing under the flares, until he launches into that great ode on the by-ways and re-
cesses of old London: "I came suddenly upon such knotty problems of alleys,
alleys without soundings . . ." Is it not a miracle, the sublime miracle of art,
that a man with words, mark you, can relate such things, which music or painting, with their much easier license of extra-intellectuality, could hardly venture
upon? To express the unutterable—furthest ideal of art. This de Quincey does
here, and in many other places. You have noticed that with exact inspiration he
has chosen nearly always to speak of London by night. Such the story, his own
life, the opium motif, Ann's fate laid on him. The vision of London, and in
their differences of all great cities, comes by night. And so:

"Oftentimes, on moonlight nights, during my first mournful abode in London, my consolation was (if such it could be thought) to gaze from Oxford
Street up every avenue in succession which pierces northwards through the heart
of Marylebone to the fields and woods."

Or that which ends:

"and by lamp-light in London, walking again with Ann—just as we had walked,
when both children, eighteen years before, along the endless terraces of Oxford
Street."

And ten more such phrases as burdened with undermeaning as an old tune; which
merely to copy out is an intoxicating pleasure; as if his words themselves had
left in them, as perfume persists on a dress, the narcotic properties of his god-
dess. Until, for the hundredth time in a lifetime, the great sweet words of the
second great apostrophe, "So then, Oxford Street, stony-hearted step-mother,"
come back in a tide into our minds. In this, with the relation of the melody to
the violin, like a virtuoso he has placed his love-story: it is one of the sort strictly
forbidden to the true artist—with which only two of them, as far as I can remember, have succeeded: Borrow and de Quincey. That is a non-sexual love,
what we used to call a Platonic love; yet nevertheless you must observe that the
girl herself, the little thin white Ann who evermore must haunt the black terraces of London nightly, bound to it as a spirit to its own true body, is a street-
walker, not a banal virgin. Just as he has incorporated great London, so has he
here seized, in this delicate and romantic episode, one of the cardinal motives of
love itself, and not the least of them. In every love, for in every love there are
somehow mystically all love-stories, there is to give it unearthly music, some

v

part of the fear of parting, some apprehension of loss, such as he himself suffered and has confided to us. Loss in time, loss in space, these are the very edge of the passionate wounds it makes.

From here, it is near to the matter of his dreams. For that loss, that infinite mislaying, is the hidden or open preoccupation of them all. De Quincey is the principal cartographer of the dream world. Not only Carie Pooter thought most dreams boring, at any rate in retrospection. I cannot see that the rigorous verbatim of psycho-analytical compilers has altered the situation. Dreams, because they are the most intimate and personal part of us, are largely incommunicable. They belong in poetry to the same class that the mystical glossolalia, which Paul sensibly condemned, does in religion. But nevertheless the dreams are the very crown of this book; the master shows himself in the conquest of the impossible. Not that the subject is not worthy. I hardly believe that there is any so deep, so necessary for mankind to muse about. For it is there that the true edge of the world we live on breaks off; there it is that the end of the raft on which we float through the mysteries that surround us dips into the surrounding sea. De Quincey, where we only jumble, leaned over and peered, long and wide eyed. We from our dreams can only bring back trivial stupidities, or at best mere hints and symbols of what we have already three-quarters forgotten. But he, just as in a line he could inscribe the infinite volume of London, so has brought back news from oblivion itself.

This world, of which he is therefore the true Columbus, is higher and deeper than any one else suspected. I have said that these prodigious travels were useful to mankind. For this world of dreams, ever so much more truly than the ether of the old concept, is the world which sustains us, with which the whole substance of our lives is permeated, and to which, above all, everyone of us has one day to return. For it is death itself and prebirth. All the secrets are there, God, and meaning, and the soul. As in a tattered papyrus, fragmentary but nevertheless as far as it goes of shining clarity, de Quincey, and he alone for all other dreams (Baudelaire's themselves beside his are legends), sets down the map. Again we are in the midst of great sonorous phrases, orchestral groupings, the very summit of expression. Hear this: "When I lay awake in bed, vast processions moved along continually in mournful pomp; friezes of never-ending stories, that to my feelings were as sad and solemn as drawn from times before Œdipus or Priam, before Tyre, before Memphis. And concurrently with this a corresponding change took place in my dreams; a theatre seemed suddenly opened and lighted up within my brain, which presented nightly spectacles of more than earthly splendour. "The whole inner resources of the possibility of man and nature seem to be glimpsed, clearly if instantaneously, in his news of the architecture, the landscapes, the lakes and "silvery expanses of water" in his dreams. Of all these dreams, the most complete is that strange fragment, equal (if there is any comparison in such heights) with the *Kubla Khan* of his friend Coleridge himself, of the Malay, of Asia, of the cosmical adventure. "I fled from the wrath of Brama through all the forests of Asia; Vishnu hated me; Seeva lay in wait for me . . ."

Here is no occasion to write of the deep complex of questions concerning the drug itself; the often contradictory opinions he himself expressed as to its share in his prodigious faculty; of its original use by him; the philosophical and even theological defence and rebuttal of its legitimate use in his case and generally for the whole of mankind; the relation of his combat with it, the tragical reproaches and sublime praise he alternately addressed to it. He has been himself clear enough, God knows. To opium at the end, as all but occasional acquaintance, he bade farewell in that tremendous Shakespearean outburst: "The sound was reverberated—everlasting farewells! and again, and yet again reverberated—everlasting farewells! And I awoke in struggles and cried aloud, 'I will sleep no more.'" There let us leave it, though reserving for secret thought perhaps many forbidden queries, such as this: apart from the unhealthfulness prejudged in the case of opium and every known narcotic—what are the rights and wrongs of drugs-using? One day, the scientists may pose the world this dreadful question in a discovery.

He died at Edinburgh, December 8th, 1859, at the age then of seventy-four. His daughter relates: "All during his illness, my father was subject to fits of delirium, though these were seldom of a painful nature. They were chiefly connected with fancies about children, and sometimes he would wander back to the days of his own childhood."

A very light, tiny man with great eyes, if you would like to know that; very shabby always, and often in the street in list slippers.

WILLIAM BOLITHO

A NOTE UPON THE TEXT

THIS EDITION embodies the text of the *Confessions of an English Opium-Eater* as Thomas de Quincey originally wrote it. The Confessions first appeared in *The London Magazine* for September & October, 1821, the Appendix in December, 1822. These parts are here reprinted exactly as they then appeared, except that various names and places left blank then are given with information acquired from later editions. In 1856 a completely revised and almost rewritten edition was published, and most reprints have been based on that edition. But Thomas de Quincey himself was dissatisfied with the revision; to his daughter he wrote: "Now that I can look back from nearly the end to the beginning, greatly I doubt whether many readers will not prefer it in its original fragmentary state."

In 1822 the Confessions were published separately for the first time with the following Notice to the Reader, dated October 1, 1821:

"The incidents recorded in the Preliminary Confessions, lie within a period of which the earlier extreme is now rather more, and the latter extreme less, than nineteen years ago: consequently, in a popular way of computing dates, many of the incidents might be indifferently referred to a distance of eighteen or of nineteen years; and, as the notes and memoranda for this narrative were drawn up originally about last Christmas, it seemed most natural in all cases to prefer the former date. In the hurry of composing the narrative, though some months had then elapsed, this date was every where retained: and, in many cases, perhaps it leads to no error, or to none of importance. But in one instance, viz. where the author speaks of his own birth-day, this adoption of one uniform date has led to a positive inaccuracy of an entire year: for, during the very time of composition, the *nineteenth* year from the earlier term of the whole period revolved to its close. It is, therefore, judged proper to mention, that the period of that narrative lies between the early part of July, 1802, and the beginning or middle of March, 1803."

In *The London Magazine* for December, 1822, the following editorial note is printed at the beginning of the Appendix to the Confessions:

"The interest excited by the two papers bearing this title, in our Numbers for September and October, 1821, will have kept our promise of a THIRD PART fresh in the remembrance of our Readers. That we are still unable to fulfil our engagement in its original meaning, will, we are sure, be matter of regret to them, as to ourselves, especially when they have perused the following affecting narrative. It was composed for the purpose of being appended to an Edition of the CONFESSIONS, in a separate Volume, which is already before the public; and we have reprinted it entire, that our Subscribers may be in possession of the whole of this extraordinary history."

"The edition of the Confessions, in a separate Volume, which is already before the public," is a duodecimo, printed for Taylor & Hessey, Fleet Street, and dated 1822. It was reprinted in the same form the year following. When de Quincey re-wrote the Confessions to make the fifth volume of the collected edition of his writings, published in 1856, the three thousand words of the original, here reprinted, spread to three times that number. In the re-writing de Quincey, who was then suffering from a painful illness, set himself to give "all that might be good in the old work, and a great deal beside that was new." Yet there is scarcely one new incident of his life. The added matter is mostly of the nature of gloss. It is in the appendix to the enlarged edition that de Quincey writes of his Norse extraction and Norman ancestry and of his remote kinship with the Quincys of America. It is in that edition also that we have the fuller information concerning his relations with his guardians, and the account of the Kelsall family, whose home he shared— the household whose "distinguishing feature . . . was the spirit of love which, under the benign superintendence of the mistress, diffused itself through all its members." "While the additions are biographically interesting," wrote Dr Richard Garnett in his edition of the Confessions, "and distinguished by great felicity in particular passages, they are as a whole detrimental to the finish and and unity which the original version possessed."

The proofs of the present edition have been carefully collated with the original text in the numbers of *The London Magazine* at the British Museum and at the Bodleian Library, Oxford. The footnotes have been restored.

The book is printed in the Centaur type, designed by Bruce Rogers.

CONFESSIONS OF AN ENGLISH OPIUM-EATER

Being an Extract from the Life of a Scholar

TO THE READER

I HERE present you, courteous reader, with the record of a remarkable period in my life: according to my application of it, I trust that it will prove, not merely an interesting record, but, in a considerable degree, useful and instructive. In *that* hope it is, that I have drawn it up: and *that* must be my apology for breaking through that delicate and honourable reserve, which, for the most part, restrains us from the public exposure of our own errors and infirmities. Nothing, indeed, is more revolting to English feelings, than the spectacle of a human being obtruding on our notice his moral ulcers or scars, and tearing away that 'decent drapery,' which time, or indulgence to human frailty, may have drawn over them: accordingly, the greater part of *our* confessions (that is, spontaneous and extra-judicial confessions) proceed from demireps, adventurers, or swindlers: and for any such acts of gratuitous self-humiliation from those who can be supposed in sympathy with the decent and self-respecting part of society, we must look to French literature, or to that part of the German, which is tainted with the spurious and defective sensibility of the French. All this I feel so forcibly, and so nervously am I alive to reproach of this tendency, that I have for many months hesitated about the propriety of allowing this, or any part of my narrative, to come before the public eye, until after my death (when, for many reasons, the whole will be published): and it is not without an anxious review of the reasons, for and against this step, that I have, at last, concluded on taking it.

Guilt and misery shrink, by a natural instinct, from public notice: they court privacy and solitude: and, even in their choice of a grave, will sometimes sequester themselves from the general population of the churchyard, as if declining to claim fellowship with the great family of man, and wishing (in the affecting language of Mr. Wordsworth)

——Humbly to express
A penitential loneliness.

It is well, upon the whole, and for the interest of us all, that it should be so: nor would I willingly, in my own person, manifest a disregard of such salutary feelings; nor in act or word do anything to weaken them. But, on the one hand, as my self-accusation does not amount to a confession of guilt, so, on the other, it is possible that, if it *did*, the benefit resulting to others, from the record of an experience purchased at so heavy a price, might compensate, by a vast overbalance, for any violence done to the feelings I have noticed, and justify a breach of the general rule. Infirmity and misery do not, of necessity, imply guilt. They approach, or recede from, the shades of that dark alliance, in proportion to the probable motives and prospects of the offender, and the palliations, known or secret, of the offence: in proportion as the temptations to it were potent from the first, and the resistance to it, in act or in effort, was earnest to the last. For my own part, without breach of truth or modesty, I may affirm, that my life has been, on the whole, the life of a philosopher: from my birth I was made an intellectual creature: and intellectual in the highest sense my pursuits and pleasures have been, even from my school-boy days. If opium-eating be a sensual pleasure, and if I am bound to confess that I have indulged in it to an excess, not yet *recorded** of any other man, it is no less true, that I have struggled against this fascinating enthralment with a religious zeal, and have, at length, accomplished what I never yet heard attributed to any other man—have untwisted, almost to its final links, the accursed chain which fettered me. Such a self-conquest may reasonably be set off in counterbalance to any kind or degree of self-indulgence. Not to insist, that in my case, the self-conquest was unquestionable, the self-indulgence open to doubts of casuistry, according as that name shall be extended to acts aiming at the bare relief of pain, or shall be restricted to such as aim at the excitement of positive pleasure.

Guilt, therefore, I do not acknowledge: and, if I did, it is possible that I might still resolve on the present act of confession, in consideration of the service which I may thereby render to the whole class of opium-eaters. But who are they? Reader, I am sorry to say, a very numerous class indeed. Of this I became con-

---

* "Not yet *recorded*," I say: for there is one celebrated man [Coleridge] of the present day, who, if all be true which is reported of him, has greatly exceeded me in quantity.

vinced some years ago, by computing, at that time, the number of those in one small class of English society (the class of men distinguished for talents, or of eminent station), who were known to me, directly or indirectly, as opium-eaters; such for instance, as the eloquent and benevolent [William Wilberforce]; the late dean of [Carlisle]; Lord [Erskine]; Mr.——, the philosopher; a late under-secretary of state (who described to me the sensation which first drove him to the use of opium, in the very same words as the dean of [Carlisle], viz. "that he felt as though rats were gnawing and abrading the coats of his stomach"); Mr. [Coleridge]; and many others, hardly less known, whom it would be tedious to mention. Now, if one class, comparatively so limited, could furnish so many scores of cases (and *that* within the knowledge of one single inquirer), it was a natural inference, that the entire population of England would furnish a proportionable number. The soundness of this inference, however, I doubted, until some facts became known to me, which satisfied me, that it was not incorrect. I will mention two: 1. Three respectable London druggists, in widely remote quarters of London, from whom I happened lately to be purchasing small quantities of opium, assured me, that the number of *amateur* opium-eaters (as I may term them) was, at this time, immense; and that the difficulty of distinguishing these persons, to whom habit had rendered opium necessary, from such as were purchasing it with a view to suicide, occasioned them daily trouble and disputes. This evidence respected London only. But, 2. (which will possibly surprise the reader more,) some years ago, on passing through Manchester, I was informed by several cotton-manufacturers, that their work-people were rapidly getting into the practice of opium-eating; so much so, that on a Saturday afternoon the counters of the druggists were strewed with pills of one, two, or three grains, in preparation for the known demand of the evening. The immediate occasion of this practice was the lowness of wages, which, at that time, would not allow them to indulge in ale or spirits: and, wages rising, it may be thought that this practice would cease: but, as I do not readily believe that any man, having once tasted the divine luxuries of opium, will afterwards descend to the gross and mortal enjoyments of alcohol, I take it for granted,

> That those eat now, who never ate before;
> And those who always ate, now eat the more.

Indeed the fascinating powers of opium are admitted, even by medical writers, who are its greatest enemies: thus, for instance, Awsiter, apothecary to Greenwich-hospital, in his "Essay on the Effects of Opium" (published in the year 1763), when attempting to explain, why Mead had not been sufficiently explicit on the

3

properties, counteragents, &c. of this drug, expresses himself in the following mysterious terms (φωνᾶντα συνετοῖσι): "perhaps he thought the subject of too delicate a nature to be made common; and as many people might then indiscriminately use it, it would take from that necessary fear and caution, which should prevent their experiencing the extensive power of this drug: *for there are many properties in it, if universally known, that would habituate the use, and make it more in request with us than the Turks themselves:* the result of which knowledge," he adds, "must prove a general misfortune." In the necessity of this conclusion I do not altogether concur: but upon that point I shall have occasion to speak at the close of my confessions, where I shall present the reader with the *moral* of my narrative.

PRELIMINARY CONFESSIONS

THESE preliminary confessions, or introductory narrative of the youthful adventures which laid the foundation of the writer's habit of opium-eating in after-life, it has been judged proper to premise, for three several reasons:

1. As forestalling that question, and giving it a satisfactory answer, which else would painfully obtrude itself in the course of the Opium-Confessions—"How came any reasonable being to subject himself to such a yoke of misery, voluntarily to incur a captivity so servile, and knowingly to fetter himself with such a seven-fold chain?"—a question which, if not somewhere plausibly resolved, could hardly fail, by the indignation which it would be apt to raise as against an act of wanton folly, to interfere with that degree of sympathy which is necessary in any case to an author's purposes.

2. As furnishing a key to some parts of that tremendous scenery which afterwards peopled the dreams of the Opium-eater.

3. As creating some previous interest of a personal sort in the confessing subject, apart from the matter of the confessions, which cannot fail to render the confessions themselves more interesting. If a man "whose talk is of oxen," should become an Opium-eater, the probability is, that (if he is not too dull to dream at all)—he will dream about oxen: whereas, in the case before him, the reader will find that the Opium-eater boasteth himself to be a philosopher; and accordingly, that the phantasmagoria of *his* dreams (waking or sleeping, day-dreams or night-dreams) is suitable to one who in that character,

Humani nihil a se alienum putat.

For amongst the conditions which he deems indispensable to the sustaining of any claim to the title of philosopher, is not merely the possession of a superb intellect in its *analytic* functions (in which part of the pretension, however, England can for some generations show but few claimants; at least, he is not aware of any known candidate for this honour who can be styled emphatically *a subtle thinker,* with the exception of *Samuel Taylor Coleridge,* and in a narrower department of thought, with the recent illustrious exception* of *David Ricardo*)—but also on

* A third exception might perhaps have been added: and my reason for not adding that exception is chiefly because it was only in his juvenile efforts that the writer whom I allude to, expressly addressed himself to philosophical themes; his riper powers having been all dedicated (on very excusable and very intelligible grounds, under the present direction of the popular mind in Eng-

5

such a constitution of the *moral* faculties, as shall give him an inner eye and power of intuition for the vision and the mysteries of our human nature: *that* constitution of faculties, in short, which (amongst all the generations of men that from the beginning of time have deployed into life, as it were, upon this planet) our English poets have possessed in the highest degree—and Scottish* Professors in the lowest.

I HAVE often been asked, how I first came to be a regular opium-eater; and have suffered, very unjustly, in the opinion of my acquaintance, from being reputed to have brought upon myself all the sufferings which I shall have to record, by a long course of indulgence in this practice purely for the sake of creating an artificial state of pleasurable excitement. This, however, is a misrepresentation of my case. True it is, that for nearly ten years I did occasionally take opium, for the sake of the exquisite pleasure it gave me: but, so long as I took it with this view, I was effectually protected from all material bad consequences, by the necessity of interposing long intervals between the several acts of indulgence, in order to renew the pleasurable sensations. It was not for the purpose of creating pleasure, but of mitigating pain in the severest degree, that I first began to use opium as an article of daily diet. In the twenty-eighth year of my age, a most painful affection of the stomach, which I had first experienced about ten years before, attacked me in great strength. This affection had originally been caused by extremities of hunger, suffered in my boyish days. During the season of hope and redundant happiness which succeeded (that is, from eighteen to twenty-four) it had slumbered: for the three following years it had revived at intervals: and now, under unfavourable circumstances, from depression of spirits, it attacked me with a violence that yielded to no remedies but opium. As the youthful sufferings, which first produced this derangement of the stomach, were interesting in themselves, and in the circumstances that attended them, I shall here briefly retrace them.

My father died, when I was about seven years old, and left me to the care of four guardians. I was sent to various schools, great and small; and was very early distinguished for my classical attainments, especially for my knowledge of Greek. At thirteen, I wrote Greek with ease; and at fifteen my command of that language was so great, that I not only composed Greek verses in lyric metres, but could converse in Greek fluently, and without embarrassment—an accomplish-

land) to criticism and the Fine Arts. This reason apart, however, I doubt whether he is not rather to be considered an acute thinker than a subtle one. It is, besides, a great drawback on his mastery over philosophical subjects, that he has obviously not had the advantage of a regular scholastic education: he has not read Plato in his youth (which most likely was only his misfortune); but neither has he read Kant in his manhood (which is his fault).

* I disclaim any allusion to *existing* professors, of whom indeed I know only one.

ment which I have not since met with in any scholar of my times, and which, in my case, was owing to the practice of daily reading off the newspapers into the best Greek I could furnish *extempore:* for the necessity of ransacking my memory and invention, for all sorts and combinations of periphrastic expressions, as equivalents for modern ideas, images, relations of things, &c. gave me a compass of diction which would never have been called out by a dull translation of moral essays, &c. "That boy," said one of my masters, pointing the attention of a stranger to me, "that boy could harangue an Athenian mob, better than you or I could address an English one." He who honoured me with this eulogy, was a scholar, "and a ripe and good one:" and of all my tutors, was the only one whom I loved or reverenced. Unfortunately for me (and, as I afterwards learned, to this worthy man's great indignation), I was transferred to the care, first of a blockhead, who was in a perpetual panic, lest I should expose his ignorance; and finally, to that of a respectable scholar, at the head of a great school on an ancient foundation. This man had been appointed to his situation by [Brasenose] College, Oxford; and was a sound, well-built scholar, but (like most men, whom I have known from that college) coarse, clumsy, and inelegant. A miserable contrast he presented, in my eyes, to the Etonian brilliancy of my favourite master: and besides, he could not disguise from my hourly notice, the poverty and meagreness of his understanding. It is a bad thing for a boy to be, and to know himself, far beyond his tutors, whether in knowledge or in power of mind. This was the case, so far as regarded knowledge at least, not with myself only: for the two boys, who jointly with myself composed the first form, were better Grecians than the headmaster, though not more elegant scholars, nor at all more accustomed to sacrifice to the graces. When I first entered, I remember that we read Sophocles; and it was a constant matter of triumph to us, the learned triumvirate of the first form, to see our 'Archididascalus' (as he loved to be called) conning our lesson before we went up, and laying a regular train, with lexicon and grammar, for blowing up and blasting (as it were) any difficulties he found in the choruses; whilst *we* never condescended to open our books, until the moment of going up, and were generally employed in writing epigrams upon his wig, or some such important matter. My two class-fellows were poor, and dependant for their future prospects at the university, on the recommendation of the head-master: but I, who had a small patrimonial property, the income of which was sufficient to support me at college, wished to be sent thither immediately. I made earnest representations on the subject to my guardians, but all to no purpose. One, who was more reasonable, and had more knowledge of the world than the rest, lived at a distance: two of the other three resigned all their authority into the hands of the fourth; and this fourth with whom I had to negotiate, was a worthy man, in his way, but haughty, obstinate, and intolerant of all opposition to his will. After a certain number of letters and personal interviews, I found that I had nothing to hope for, not even a compromise of the matter, from my guardian: unconditional submission was what he demanded: and I prepared myself, therefore, for other measures. Summer was now coming on with hasty steps, and my seventeenth birth-day was fast approaching; after which day I had sworn within myself, that I would no longer be numbered amongst school-boys. Money being what I chiefly wanted, I wrote to a woman of high rank, who, though young herself, had known me from a child, and had latterly treated me with great distinction, requesting that she would 'lend' me five guineas. For upwards of a week no answer came; and I was beginning to despond, when, at length, a servant put into my hands a double letter, with a coronet on the seal. The letter was kind and obliging: the fair writer was on the sea-coast, and in that way the delay had arisen: she inclosed double of what I had asked, and good-naturedly hinted, that if I should *never* repay her, it would not absolutely ruin her. Now then, I was prepared for my scheme: ten guineas, added to about two which I had remaining from my pocket money, seemed to me sufficient for an indefinite length of time: and at that happy age, if no *definite* boundary can be assigned to one's power, the spirit of hope and pleasure makes it virtually infinite.

It is a just remark of Dr. Johnson's (and what cannot often be said of his remarks, it is a very feeling one), that we never do any thing consciously for the last time (of things, that is, which we have long been in the habit of doing) without sadness of heart. This truth I felt deeply, when I came to leave [Manchester], a place which I did not love, and where I had not been happy. On the evening before I left [Manchester] for ever, I grieved when the ancient and lofty school-room resounded with the evening service, performed for the last time in my hearing; and at night, when the muster-roll of names was called over, and mine (as usual) was called first, I stepped forward, and, passing the head-master, who was standing by, I bowed to him, and looked earnestly in his face, thinking to myself, 'He is old and infirm, and in this world I shall not see him again.' I was right: I never *did* see him again, nor ever shall. He looked at me complacently, smiled good-naturedly, returned my salutation (or rather, my valediction), and we parted (though he knew it not) for ever. I could not reverence him intellectually: but he had been uniformly kind to me, and had allowed me many indulgencies: and I grieved at the thought of the mortification I should inflict upon him.

The morning came, which was to launch me into the world, and from which my whole succeeding life has, in many important points, taken its colouring. I

8

lodged in the head-master's house, and had been allowed, from my first entrance, the indulgence of a private room, which I used both as a sleeping room and as a study. At half after three I rose, and gazed with deep emotion at the ancient towers of [the collegiate church], 'drest in earliest light,' and beginning to crimson with the radiant lustre of a cloudless July morning. I was firm and immoveable in my purpose: but yet agitated by anticipation of uncertain danger and troubles; and, if I could have foreseen the hurricane, and perfect hail-storm of affliction which soon fell upon me, well might I have been agitated. To this agitation the deep peace of the morning presented an affecting contrast, and in some degree a medicine. The silence was more profound than that of midnight: and to me the silence of a summer morning is more touching than all other silence, because, the light being broad and strong, as that of noon-day at other seasons of the year, it seems to differ from perfect day, chiefly because man is not yet abroad; and thus, the peace of nature, and of the innocent creatures of God, seems to be secure and deep, only so long as the presence of man, and his restless and unquiet spirit, are not there to trouble its sanctity. I dressed myself, took my hat and gloves, and lingered a little in the room. For the last year and a half this room had been my 'pensive citadel:' here I had read and studied through all the hours of night: and, though true it was, that for the latter part of this time I, who was framed for love and gentle affections, had lost my gaiety and happiness, during the strife and fever of contention with my guardian; yet, on the other hand, as a boy, so passionately fond of books, and dedicated to intellectual pursuits, I could not fail to have enjoyed many happy hours in the midst of general dejection. I wept as I looked round on the chair, hearth, writing-table, and other familiar objects, knowing too certainly, that I looked upon them for the last time. Whilst I write this, it is eighteen years ago; and yet, at this moment, I see distinctly as if it were yesterday, the lineaments and expression of the object on which I fixed my parting gaze: it was a picture of the lovely ——, which hung over the mantle-piece; the eyes and mouth of which were so beautiful, and the whole countenance so radiant with benignity, and divine tranquillity, that I had a thousand times laid down my pen, or my book, to gather consolation from it, as a devotee from his patron saint. Whilst I was yet gazing upon it, the deep tones of [Manchester] clock proclaimed that it was four o'clock. I went up to the picture, kissed it, and then gently walked out, and closed the door for ever!

— —

So blended and intertwisted in this life are occasions of laughter and of tears, that I cannot yet recal, without smiling, an incident which occurred at that time, and which had nearly put a stop to the immediate execution of my plan. I had a trunk of immense weight; for, besides my clothes, it contained nearly all my library. The difficulty was to get this removed to a carrier's: my room was at an aërial elevation in the house, and (what was worse) the stair-case, which communicated with this angle of the building, was accessible only by a gallery, which passed the head-master's chamber-door. I was a favourite with all the servants; and, knowing that any of them would screen me, and act confidentially, I communicated my embarrassment to a groom of the head-master's. The groom swore he would do anything I wished; and, when the time arrived, went up stairs to bring the trunk down. This I feared was beyond the strength of any one man: however, the groom was a man—

> Of Atlantean shoulders, fit to bear
> The weight of mightiest monarchies;

and had a back as spacious as Salisbury plain. Accordingly he persisted in bringing down the trunk alone, whilst I stood waiting at the foot of the last flight, in anxiety for the event. For some time I heard him descending with slow and firm steps: but, unfortunately, from his trepidation, as he drew near the dangerous quarter, within a few steps of the gallery, his foot slipped; and the mighty burden falling from his shoulders, gained such increase of impetus at each step of the descent, that, on reaching the bottom, it trundled, or rather leaped, right across, with the noise of twenty devils, against the very bed-room door of the archididascalus. My first thought was, that all was lost; and that my only chance for executing a retreat was to sacrifice my baggage. However, on reflection, I determined to abide the issue. The groom was in the utmost alarm, both on his own account and on mine: but, in spite of this, so irresistibly had the sense of the ludicrous, in this unhappy *contretems*, taken possession of his fancy, that he sang out a long, loud, and canorous peal of laughter, that might have wakened the Seven Sleepers. At the sound of this resonant merriment, within the very ears of insulted authority, I could not myself forbear joining in it: subdued to this, not so much by the unhappy *étourderie* of the trunk, as by the effect it had upon the groom. We both expected, as a matter of course, that Dr. [Lawson] would sally out of his room: for, in general, if but a mouse stirred, he sprang out like a mastiff from his kennel. Strange to say, however, on this occasion, when the noise of laughter had ceased, no sound, or rustling even, was to be heard in the bed-room. Dr. [Lawson] had a painful complaint, which, sometimes keeping him awake, made his sleep, perhaps, when it *did* come, the deeper. Gathering courage from the silence, the groom hoisted his burden again, and accomplished the remainder of his descent without accident. I waited until I saw the trunk placed on

a wheel-barrow, and on its road to the carrier's: then, 'with Providence my guide,' I set off on foot,—carrying a small parcel, with some articles of dress, under my arm; a favourite English poet in one pocket; and a small 12mo. volume, containing about nine plays of Euripides, in the other.

It had been my intention originally to proceed to Westmoreland, both from the love I bore to that county, and on other personal accounts. Accident, however, gave a different direction to my wanderings, and I bent my steps towards North Wales.

After wandering about for some time in Denbighshire, Merionethshire, and Caernarvonshire, I took lodgings in a small neat house in B[angor]. Here I might have staid with great comfort for many weeks; for, provisions were cheap at B[angor], from the scarcity of other markets for the surplus produce of a wide agricultural district. An accident, however, in which, perhaps, no offence was designed, drove me out to wander again. I know not whether my reader may have remarked, but *I* have often remarked, that the proudest class of people in England (or at any rate, the class whose pride is most apparent) are the families of bishops. Noblemen, and their children, carry about with them, in their very titles, a sufficient notification of their rank. Nay, their very names (and this applies also to the children of many untitled houses) are often, to the English ear, adequate exponents of high birth, or descent. Sackville, Manners, Fitzroy, Paulet, Cavendish, and scores of others, tell their own tale. Such persons, therefore, find every where a due sense of their claims already established, except among those who are ignorant of the world, by virtue of their own obscurity: 'Not to know *them*, argues one's self unknown.' Their manners take a suitable tone and colouring; and, for once that they find it necessary to impress a sense of their consequence upon others, they meet with a thousand occasions for moderating and tempering this sense by acts of courteous condescension. With the families of bishops it is otherwise: with them it is all up-hill work, to make known their pretensions: for the proportion of the episcopal bench, taken from noble families, is not at any time very large; and the succession to these dignities is so rapid, that the public ear seldom has time to become familiar with them, unless where they are connected with some literary reputation. Hence it is, that the children of bishops carry about with them an austere and repulsive air, indicative of claims not generally acknowledged, a sort of *noli me tangere* manner, nervously apprehensive of too familiar approach, and shrinking with the sensitiveness of a gouty man, from all contact with the οἱ πολλοί. Doubtless, a powerful understanding, or unusual goodness of nature, will preserve a man from such weakness: but, in general, the truth of my representation will be acknowledged: pride, if not of deeper

11

root in such families, appears, at least, more upon the surface of their manners. This spirit of manners naturally communicates itself to their domestics, and other dependants. Now, my landlady had been a lady's maid, or a nurse, in the family of the Bishop of [Bangor]; and had but lately married away and 'settled' (as such people express it) for life. In a little town like B[angor], merely to have lived in the bishop's family, conferred some distinction: and my good landlady had rather more than her share of the pride I have noticed on that score. What 'my lord' said, and what 'my lord' did, how useful he was in parliament, and how indispensable at Oxford, formed the daily burden of her talk. All this I bore very well: for I was too good-natured to laugh in anybody's face, and I could make an ample allowance for the garrulity of an old servant. Of necessity, however, I must have appeared in her eyes very inadequately impressed with the bishop's importance: and, perhaps, to punish me for my indifference, or possibly by accident, she one day repeated to me a conversation in which I was indirectly a party concerned. She had been to the palace to pay her respects to the family; and, dinner being over, was summoned into the dining-room. In giving an account of her household economy, she happened to mention, that she had let her apartments. Thereupon the good bishop (it seemed) had taken occasion to caution her as to her selection of inmates: 'for,' said he, 'you must recollect, Betty, that this place is in the high road to the Head; so that multitudes of Irish swindlers, running away from their debts into England—and of English swindlers, running away from their debts to the Isle of Man, are likely to take this place in their route.' This advice was certainly not without reasonable grounds: but rather fitted to be stored up for Mrs. Betty's private meditations, than specially reported to me. What followed, however, was somewhat worse:—'Oh, my lord,' answered my landlady (according to her own representation of the matter), 'I really don't think this young gentleman is a swindler; because ——': 'You don't *think* me a swindler?' said I, interrupting her, in a tumult of indignation: 'for the future I shall spare you the trouble of thinking about it.' And without delay I prepared for my departure. Some concessions the good woman seemed disposed to make: but a harsh and contemptuous expression, which I fear that I applied to the learned dignitary himself, roused *her* indignation in turn: and reconciliation then became impossible. I was, indeed, greatly irritated at the bishop's having suggested any grounds of suspicion, however remotely, against a person whom he had never seen: and I thought of letting him know my mind in Greek: which, at the same time that it would furnish some presumption that I was no swindler, would also (I hoped) compel the bishop to reply in the same language; in which case, I doubted not to make it appear, that if I was not so rich as his lordship, I

12

was a far better Grecian. Calmer thoughts, however, drove this boyish design out of my mind: for I considered, that the bishop was in the right to counsel an old servant; that he could not have designed that his advice should be reported to me; and that the same coarseness of mind, which had led Mrs. Betty to repeat the advice at all, might have coloured it in a way more agreeable to her own style of thinking, than to the actual expressions of the worthy bishop.

I left the lodgings the very same hour; and this turned out a very unfortunate occurrence for me: because, living henceforward at inns, I was drained of my money very rapidly. In a fortnight I was reduced to short allowance; that is, I could allow myself only one meal a-day. From the keen appetite produced by constant exercise, and mountain air, acting on a youthful stomach, I soon began to suffer greatly on this slender regimen; for the single meal, which I could venture to order, was coffee or tea. Even this, however, was at length withdrawn: and afterwards, so long as I remained in Wales, I subsisted either on blackberries, hips, haws, &c. or on the casual hospitalities which I now and then received, in return for such little services as I had an opportunity of rendering. Sometimes I wrote letters of business for cottagers, who happened to have relatives in Liverpool, or in London: more often I wrote love-letters to their sweethearts for young women who had lived as servants in Shrewsbury, or other towns on the English border. On all such occasions I gave great satisfaction to my humble friends, and was generally treated with hospitality: and once, in particular, near the village of Llan-y-styndw (or some such name), in a sequestered part of Merionethshire, I was entertained for upwards of three days by a family of young people, with an affectionate and fraternal kindness that left an impression upon my heart not yet impaired. The family consisted, at that time, of four sisters, and three brothers, all grown up, and all remarkable for elegance and delicacy of manners. So much beauty, and so much native good-breeding and refinement, I do not remember to have seen before or since in any cottage, except once or twice in Westmorland and Devonshire. They spoke English: an accomplishment not often met with in so many members of one family, especially in villages remote from the high-road. Here I wrote, on my first introduction, a letter about prize-money, for one of the brothers, who had served on board an English man of war; and more privately, two love-letters for two of the sisters. They were both interesting looking girls, and one of uncommon loveliness. In the midst of their confusion and blushes, whilst dictating, or rather giving me general instructions, it did not require any great penetration to discover that what they wished was, that their letters should be as kind as was consistent with proper maidenly pride. I contrived so to temper my expressions, as to reconcile the gratification of both feelings: and they were

13

as much pleased with the way in which I had expressed their thoughts, as (in their simplicity) they were astonished at my having so readily discovered them. The reception one meets with from the women of a family, generally determines the tenor of one's whole entertainment. In this case, I had discharged my confidential duties as secretary, so much to the general satisfaction, perhaps also amusing them with my conversation, that I was pressed to stay with a cordiality which I had little inclination to resist. I slept with the brothers, the only unoccupied bed standing in the apartment of the young women: but in all other points, they treated me with a respect not usually paid to purses as light as mine; as if my scholarship were sufficient evidence, that I was of "gentle blood." Thus I lived with them for three days, and great part of a fourth: and, from the undiminished kindness which they continued to show me, I believe I might have staid with them up to this time, if their power had corresponded with their wishes. On the last morning, however, I perceived upon their countenances, as they sate at break-fast, the expression of some unpleasant communication which was at hand; and soon after one of the brothers explained to me that their parents had gone, the day before my arrival, to an annual meeting of Methodists, held at Caernarvon, and were that day expected to return; "and if they should not be so civil as they ought to be," he begged, on the part of all the young people, that I would not take it amiss. The parents returned, with churlish faces, and "*Dym Sassenach*" (*no English*), in answer to all my addresses. I saw how matters stood; and so, taking an affectionate leave of my kind and interesting young hosts, I went my way. For, though they spoke warmly to their parents in my behalf, and often excused the manner of the old people, by saying, that it was "only their way," yet I easily understood that my talent for writing love-letters would do as little to recommend me, with two grave sexagenarian Welsh Methodists, as my Greek Sapphics or Alcaics: and what had been hospitality, when offered to me with the gracious courtesy of my young friends, would become charity, when connected with the harsh demeanour of these old people. Certainly, Mr. Shelley is right in his notions about old age: unless powerfully counteracted by all sorts of oppo-site agencies, it is a miserable corrupter and blighter to the genial charities of the human heart.

Soon after this, I contrived, by means which I must omit for want of room, to transfer myself to London. And now began the latter and fiercer stage of my long-sufferings: without using a disproportionate expression I might say, of my agony. For I now suffered, for upwards of sixteen weeks, the physical anguish of hunger in various degrees of intensity; but as bitter, perhaps, as ever any human being can have suffered who has survived it. I would not needlessly harass my

14

reader's feelings, by a detail of all that I endured: for extremities such as these, under any circumstances of heaviest misconduct or guilt, cannot be contemplated, even in description, without a rueful pity that is painful to the natural goodness of the human heart. Let it suffice, at least on this occasion, to say, that a few fragments of bread from the breakfast-table of one individual (who supposed me to be ill, but did not know of my being in utter want), and these at uncertain intervals, constituted my whole support. During the former part of my sufferings (that is, generally in Wales, and always for the first two months in London) I was houseless, and very seldom slept under a roof. To this constant exposure to the open air I ascribe it mainly, that I did not sink under my torments. Latterly, however, when colder and more inclement weather came on, and when, from the length of my sufferings, I had begun to sink into a more languishing condition, it was, no doubt, fortunate for me, that the same person to whose breakfast-table I had access, allowed me to sleep in a large unoccupied house, of which he was tenant. Unoccupied, I call it, for there was no household or establishment in it; nor any furniture, indeed, except a table, and a few chairs. But I found, on taking possession of my new quarters, that the house already contained one single inmate, a poor friendless child, apparently ten years old; but she seemed hunger-bitten; and sufferings of that sort often make children look older than they are. From this forlorn child I learned, that she had slept and lived there alone, for some time before I came: and great joy the poor creature expressed, when she found that I was, in future, to be her companion through the hours of darkness. The house was large; and, from the want of furniture, the noise of the rats made a prodigious echoing on the spacious stair-case and hall; and, amidst the real fleshly ills of cold, and, I fear, hunger, the forsaken child had found leisure to suffer still more (it appeared) from the self-created one of ghosts. I promised her protection against all ghosts whatsoever: but, alas! I could offer her no other assistance. We lay upon the floor, with a bundle of cursed law papers for a pillow: but with no other covering than a sort of large horseman's cloak: afterwards, however, we discovered, in a garret, an old sopha-cover, a small piece of rug, and some fragments of other articles, which added a little to our warmth. The poor child crept close to me for warmth, and for security against her ghostly enemies. When I was not more than usually ill, I took her into my arms, so that, in general, she was tolerably warm, and often slept when I could not: for, during the last two months of my sufferings, I slept much in the day-time, and was apt to fall into transient dozings at all hours. But my sleep distressed me more than my watching: for, besides the tumultuousness of my dreams (which were only not so awful as those which I shall have to describe hereafter as produced by opium),

15

my sleep was never more than what is called *dog-sleep*; so that I could hear myself moaning, and was often, as it seemed to me, wakened suddenly by my own voice; and, about this time, a hideous sensation began to haunt me as soon as I fell into a slumber, which has since returned upon me, at different periods of my life, viz. a sort of twitching (I know not where, but apparently about the region of the stomach), which compelled me violently to throw out my feet for the sake of relieving it. This sensation coming on as soon as I began to sleep, and the effort to relieve it constantly awaking me, at length I slept only from exhaustion; and from increasing weakness (as I said before) I was constantly falling asleep, and constantly awaking. Meantime, the master of the house sometimes came in upon us suddenly, and very early, sometimes not till ten o'clock, sometimes not at all. He was in constant fear of bailiffs: improving on the plan of Cromwell, every night he slept in a different quarter of London; and I observed that he never failed to examine, through a private window, the appearance of those who knocked at the door, before he would allow it to be opened. He breakfasted alone: indeed, his tea equipage would hardly have admitted of his hazarding an invitation to a second person—any more than the quantity of esculent *matériel*, which, for the most part, was little more than a roll, or a few biscuits, which he had bought on his road from the place where he had slept. Or, if he *had* asked a party, as I once learnedly and facetiously observed to him—the several members of it must have *stood* in the relation to each other (not *sate* in any relation whatever) of succession, as the metaphysicians have it, and not of co-existence; in the relation of the parts of time, and not of the parts of space. During his breakfast, I generally contrived a reason for lounging in; and, with an air of as much indifference as I could assume, took up such fragments as he had left—sometimes, indeed, there were none at all. In doing this, I committed no robbery except upon the man himself, who was thus obliged (I believe) now and then to send out at noon for an extra biscuit; for, as to the poor child, *she* was never admitted into his study (if I may give that name to his chief depositary of parchments, law writings, &c.); that room was to her the Blue-beard room of the house, being regularly locked on his departure to dinner, about six o'clock, which usually was his final departure for the night. Whether this child were an illegitimate daughter of Mr. [Brunell], or only a servant, I could not ascertain; she did not herself know; but certainly she was treated altogether as a menial servant. No sooner did Mr. [Brunell] make his appearance, than she went below stairs, brushed his shoes, coat, &c.; and, except when she was summoned to run an errand, she never emerged from the dismal Tartarus of the kitchens, &c. to the upper air, until my welcome knock at night called up her little trembling foot-

16

steps to the front door. Of her life during the day-time, however, I knew little but what I gathered from her own account at night; for, as soon as the hours of business commenced, I saw that my absence would be acceptable; and, in general, therefore, I went off and sate in the parks, or elsewhere, until night-fall.

But who, and what, meantime, was the master of the house himself? Reader, he was one of those anomalous practitioners in lower departments of the law, who—what shall I say?—who, on prudential reasons, or from necessity, deny themselves all indulgence in the luxury of too delicate a conscience: (a periphrasis which might be abridged considerably, but *that* I leave to the reader's taste:) in many walks of life, a conscience is a more expensive incumbrance, than a wife or a carriage; and just as people talk of "laying down" their carriages, so I suppose my friend, Mr. [Brunell] had "laid down" his conscience for a time; meaning, doubtless, to resume it as soon as he could afford it. The inner economy of such a man's daily life would present a most strange picture, if I could allow myself to amuse the reader at his expense. Even with my limited opportunities for observing what went on, I saw many scenes of London intrigues, and complex chicanery, "cycle and epicycle, orb in orb," at which I sometimes smile to this day—and at which I smiled then, in spite of my misery. My situation, however, at that time, gave me little experience, in my own person, of any qualities in Mr. [Brunell]'s character but such as did him honour; and of his whole strange composition, I must forget every thing but that towards me he was obliging, and, to the extent of his power, generous.

That power was not, indeed, very extensive; however, in common with the rats, I sate rent free; and, as Dr. Johnson has recorded, that he never but once in his life had as much wall-fruit as he could eat, so let me be grateful, that on that single occasion I had as large a choice of apartments in a London mansion as I could possibly desire. Except the Blue-beard room, which the poor child believed to be haunted, all others, from the attics to the cellars, were at our service; "the world was all before us;" and we pitched our tent for the night in any spot we chose. This house I have already described as a large one; it stands in a conspicuous situation, and in a well-known part of London. Many of my readers will have passed it, I doubt not, within a few hours of reading this. For myself, I never fail to visit it when business draws me to London; about ten o'clock, this very night, August 15, 1821, being my birth-day,—I turned aside from my evening walk, down Oxford-street, purposely to take a glance at it: it is now occupied by a respectable family; and, by the lights in the front drawing-room, I observed a domestic party, assembled perhaps at tea, and apparently cheerful and gay. Marvellous contrast in my eyes to the darkness—cold—silence—and desolation of that same house eighteen years ago, when its nightly occupants were one famishing scholar, and a neglected child.—Her, by the bye, in after years, I vainly endeavoured to trace. Apart from her situation, she was not what would be called an interesting child: she was neither pretty, nor quick in understanding, nor remarkably pleasing in manners. But, thank God! even in those years I needed not the embellishments of novel-accessaries to conciliate my affections; plain human nature, in its humblest and most homely apparel, was enough for me: and I loved the child because she was my partner in wretchedness. If she is now living, she is probably a mother, with children of her own; but, as I have said, I could never trace her.

This I regret, but another person there was at that time, whom I have since sought to trace with far deeper earnestness, and with far deeper sorrow at my failure. This person was a young woman, and one of that unhappy class who subsist upon the wages of prostitution. I feel no shame, nor have any reason to feel it, in avowing, that I was then on familiar and friendly terms with many women in that unfortunate condition. The reader needs neither smile at this avowal, nor frown. For, not to remind my classical readers of the old Latin proverb— 'Sine Cerere,' &c., it may well be supposed that in the existing state of my purse, my connexion with such women could not have been an impure one. But the truth is, that at no time of my life have I been a person to hold myself polluted by the touch or approach of any creature that wore a human shape: on the contrary, from my very earliest youth it has been my pride to converse familiarly, more Socratico, with all human beings, man, woman, and child, that chance might fling in my way: a practice which is friendly to the knowledge of human nature, to good feelings, and to that frankness of address which becomes a man who would be thought a philosopher. For a philosopher should not see with the eyes of the poor limitary creature calling himself a man of the world, and filled with narrow and self-regarding prejudices of birth and education, but should look upon himself as a Catholic creature, and as standing in an equal relation to high and low—to educated and uneducated, to the guilty and the innocent. Being myself at that time of necessity a peripatetic, or a walker of the streets, I naturally fell in more frequently with those female peripetetics who are technically called Street-walkers. Many of these women had occasionally taken my part against watchmen who wished to drive me off the steps of houses where I was sitting. But one amongst them, the one on whose account I have at all introduced this subject—yet no! let me not class thee, Oh noble minded Ann ——, with that order of women; let me find, if it be possible, some gentler name to designate the condition of her to whose bounty and compassion, ministering to my neces-

18

sities when all the world had forsaken me, I owe it that I am at this time alive.—
For many weeks I had walked at nights with this poor friendless girl up and down Oxford Street, or had rested with her on steps and under the shelter of porticos. She could not be so old as myself: she told me, indeed, that she had not completed her sixteenth year. By such questions as my interest about her prompted, I had gradually drawn forth her simple history. Hers was a case of ordinary occurrence (as I have since had reason to think), and one in which, if London beneficence had better adapted its arrangements to meet it, the power of the law might oftener be interposed to protect, and to avenge. But the stream of London charity flows in a channel which, though deep and mighty, is yet noiseless and underground; not obvious or readily accessible to poor houseless wanderers; and it cannot be denied that the outside air and frame-work of London society is harsh, cruel, and repulsive. In any case, however, I saw that part of her injuries might easily have been redressed; and I urged her often and earnestly to lay her complaint before a magistrate: friendless as she was, I assured her that she would meet with immediate attention; and that English justice, which was no respecter of persons, would speedily and amply avenge her on the brutal ruffian who had plundered her little property. She promised me often that she would; but she delayed taking the steps I pointed out from time to time: for she was timid and dejected to a degree which showed how deeply sorrow had taken hold of her young heart: and perhaps she thought justly that the most upright judge, and the most righteous tribunals, could do nothing to repair her heaviest wrongs. Something, however, would perhaps have been done: for it had been settled between us at length, but unhappily on the very last time but one that I was ever to see her, that in a day or two we should go together before a magistrate, and that I should speak on her behalf. This little service it was destined, however, that I should never realise. Meantime, that which she rendered to me, and which was greater than I could ever have repaid her, was this:—One night, when we were pacing slowly along Oxford Street, and after a day when I had felt more than usually ill and faint, I requested her to turn off with me into Soho Square: thither we went; and we sate down on the steps of a house, which, to this hour, I never pass without a pang of grief, and an inner act of homage to the spirit of that unhappy girl, in memory of the noble action which she there performed. Suddenly, as we sate, I grew much worse: I had been leaning my head against her bosom; and all at once I sank from her arms and fell backwards on the steps. From the sensations I then had, I felt an inner conviction of the liveliest kind that without some powerful and reviving stimulus, I should either have died on the spot—or should at least have sunk to a point of exhaustion from which all reäscent under my friendless

19

circumstances would soon have become hopeless. Then it was, at this crisis of my fate, that my poor orphan companion—who had herself met with little but injuries in this world—stretched out a saving hand to me. Uttering a cry of terror, but without a moment's delay, she ran off into Oxford Street, and in less time than could be imagined, returned to me with a glass of port wine and spices, that acted upon my empty stomach (which at that time would have rejected all solid food) with an instantaneous power of restoration: and for this glass the generous girl without a murmur paid out of her own humble purse at a time—be it remembered!—when she had scarcely wherewithal to purchase the bare necessaries of life, and when she could have no reason to expect that I should ever be able to reimburse her.—Oh! youthful benefactress! how often in succeeding years, standing in solitary places, and thinking of thee with grief of heart and perfect love, how often have I wished that, as in ancient times the curse of a father was believed to have a supernatural power, and to pursue its object with a fatal necessity of self-fulfilment,—even so the benediction of a heart oppressed with gratitude, might have a like prerogative; might have power given to it from above to chace —to haunt—to way-lay—to overtake—to pursue thee into the central darkness of a London brothel, or (if it were possible) into the darkness of the grave—there to awaken thee with an authentic message of peace and forgiveness, and of final reconciliation!

I do not often weep: for not only do my thoughts on subjects connected with the chief interests of man daily, nay hourly, descend a thousand fathoms "too deep for tears;" not only does the sternness of my habits of thought present an antagonism to the feelings which prompt tears—wanting of necessity to those who, being protected usually by their levity from any tendency to meditative sorrow, would by that same levity be made incapable of resisting it on any casual access of such feelings:—but also, I believe that all minds which have contemplated such objects as deeply as I have done, must, for their own protection from utter despondency, have early encouraged and cherished some tranquillizing belief as to the future balances and the hieroglyphic meanings of human sufferings. On these accounts, I am cheerful to this hour: and, as I have said, I do not often weep. Yet some feelings, though not deeper or more passionate, are more tender than others: and often, when I walk at this time in Oxford Street by dreamy lamp-light, and hear those airs played on a barrel-organ which years ago solaced me and my dear companion (as I must always call her) I shed tears, and muse with myself at the mysterious dispensation which so suddenly and so critically separated us for ever. How it happened, the reader will understand from what what remains of this introductory narration.

20

Soon after the period of the last incident I have recorded, I met, in Albemarle Street, a gentleman of his late Majesty's household. This gentleman had received hospitalities, on different occasions, from my family: and he challenged me upon the strength of my family likeness. I did not attempt any disguise: I answered his questions ingenuously,—and, on his pledging his word of honor that he would not betray me to my guardians, I gave him an address to my friend the Attorney's. The next day I received from him a 10*l*. Bank-note. The letter inclosing it was delivered with other letters of business to the Attorney: but, though his look and manner informed me that he suspected its contents, he gave it up to me honorably and without demur.

This present, from the particular service to which it was applied, leads me naturally to speak of the purpose which had allured me up to London, and which I had been (to use a forensic word) *soliciting* from the first day of my arrival in London, to that of my final departure.

In so mighty a world as London, it will surprise my readers that I should not have found some means of staving off the last extremities of penury: and it will strike them that two resources at least must have been open to me,—viz. either to seek assistance from the friends of my family, or to turn my youthful talents and attainments into some channel of pecuniary emolument. As to the first course, I may observe, generally, that what I dreaded beyond all other evils was the chance of being reclaimed by my guardians; not doubting that whatever power the law gave them would have been enforced against me to the utmost; that is, to the extremity of forcibly restoring me to the school which I had quitted: a restoration which as it would in my eyes have been a dishonor, even if submitted to voluntarily, could not fail, when extorted from me in contempt and defiance of my known wishes and efforts, to have been a humiliation worse to me than death, and which would indeed have terminated in death. I was, therefore, shy enough of applying for assistance even in those quarters where I was sure of receiving it—at the risk of furnishing my guardians with any clue for recovering me. But, as to London in particular, though, doubtless, my father had in his life-time had many friends there, yet (as ten years had passed since his death) I remembered few of them even by name: and never having seen London before, except once for a few hours, I knew not the address of even those few. To this mode of gaining help, therefore, in part the difficulty, but much more the paramount fear which I have mentioned, habitually indisposed me. In regard to the other mode, I now feel half inclined to join my reader in wondering that I should have overlooked it. As a corrector of Greek proofs (if in no other way), I might doubtless have gained enough for my slender wants. Such an office as this I could have discharged with an exemplary and punctual accuracy that would soon have gained me the confidence of my employers. But it must not be forgotten that, even for such an office as this, it was necessary that I should first of all have an introduction to some respectable publisher: and this I had no means of obtaining. To say the truth, however, it had never once occurred to me to think of literary labours as a source of profit. No mode sufficiently speedy of obtaining money had ever occurred to me, but that of borrowing it on the strength of my future claims and expectations. This mode I sought by every avenue to compass: and amongst other persons I applied to a Jew named D[ell].*

To this Jew, and to other advertising money-lenders (some of whom were, I believe, also Jews), I had introduced myself with an account of my expectations; which account, on examining my father's will at Doctor's Commons, they had ascertained to be correct. The person there mentioned as the second son of [Thomas Quincey], was found to have all the claims (or more than all) that I had stated: but one question still remained, which the faces of the Jews pretty significantly suggested,—was *I* that person? This doubt had never occurred to me as a possible one: I had rather feared, whenever my Jewish friends scrutinized me keenly, that I might be too well known to be that person—and that some scheme might be passing in their minds for entrapping me and selling me to my guardians. It was strange to me to find my own self, *materialiter* considered (so I expressed it, for I doated on logical accuracy of distinctions), accused, or at least suspected, of counterfeiting my own self, *formaliter* considered. However, to satisfy their scruples, I took the only course in my power. Whilst I was in

---

* To this same Jew, by the way, some eighteen months afterwards, I applied again on the same business; and, dating at that time from a respectable college, I was fortunate enough to gain his serious attention to my proposals. My necessities had not arisen from any extravagance, or youthful levities (these my habits and the nature of my pleasures raised me far above), but simply from the vindictive malice of my guardian, who, when he found himself no longer able to prevent me from going to the university, had, as a parting token of his good nature, refused to sign an order for granting me a shilling beyond the allowance made to me at school—viz. 100*l.* per ann. Upon this sum it was, in my time, barely possible to have lived in college; and not possible to a man who, though above the paltry affectation of ostentatious disregard for money, and without any expensive tastes, confided nevertheless rather too much in servants, and did not delight in the petty details of minute economy. I soon, therefore, became embarrassed: and at length, after a most voluminous negotiation with the Jew, (some parts of which, if I had leisure to rehearse them, would greatly amuse my readers), I was put in possession of the sum I asked for—on the 'regular' terms of paying the Jew seventeen and a half per cent. by way of annuity on all the money furnished; Israel, on his part, graciously resuming no more than about ninety guineas of the said money, on account of an Attorney's bill, (for what services, to whom rendered, and when, whether at the siege of Jerusalem—at the building of the Second Temple—or on some earlier occasion, I have not yet been able to discover). How many perches this bill measured I really forget: but I still keep it in a cabinet of natural curiosities; and sometime or other I believe I shall present it to the British Museum.

Wales, I had received various letters from young friends: these I produced: for I carried them constantly in my pocket—being, indeed, by this time, almost the only relics of my personal incumbrances (excepting the clothes I wore) which I had not in one way or other disposed of. Most of these letters were from the Earl of [Altamont], who was at that time my chief (or rather only) confidential friend. These letters were dated from Eton. I had also some from the Marquis of [Sligo], his father, who, though absorbed in agricultural pursuits, yet having been an Etonian himself, and as good a scholar as a nobleman needs to be—still retained an affection for classical studies, and for youthful scholars. He had, accordingly, from the time that I was fifteen, corresponded with me; sometimes upon the great improvements which he had made, or was meditating, in the counties of M[ayo] and Sl[igo] since I had been there; sometimes upon the merits of a Latin poet; at other times, suggesting subjects to me on which he wished me to write verses.

On reading the letters, one of my Jewish friends agreed to furnish two or three hundred pounds on my personal security—provided I could persuade the young Earl, who was, by the way, not older than myself, to guarantee the payment on our coming of age: the Jew's final object being, as I now suppose, not the trifling profit he could expect to make by me, but the prospect of establishing a connection with my noble friend, whose immense expectations were well known to him. In pursuance of this proposal on the part of the Jew, about eight or nine days after I had received the 10*l.*, I prepared to go down to Eton. Nearly 3*l.* of the money I had given to my money-lending friend, on his alleging that the stamps must be bought, in order that the writings might be preparing whilst I was away from London. I thought in my heart that he was lying; but I did not wish to give him any excuse for charging his own delays upon me. A smaller sum I had given to my friend the attorney (who was connected with the money-lenders as their lawyer), to which, indeed, he was entitled for his unfurnished lodgings. About fifteen shillings I had employed in re-establishing (though in a very humble way) my dress. Of the remainder I gave one quarter to Ann, meaning on my return to have divided with her whatever might remain. These arrangements made,—soon after six o'clock, on a dark winter evening, I set off, accompanied by Ann, towards Piccadilly; for it was my intention to go down as far as Salthill on the Bath or Bristol Mail. Our course lay through a part of the town which has now all disappeared, so that I can no longer retrace its ancient boundaries: Swallow-street, I think it was called. Having time enough before us, however, we bore away to the left until we came into Golden-square: there, near the corner of Sherrard-street, we sat down; not wishing to part in the tumult and blaze of Piccadilly. I had told her of my plans some time before: and I now assured her again that she should share in my good fortune, if I met with any; and that I would never forsake her, as soon as I had power to protect her. This I fully intended, as much from inclination as from a sense of duty: for, setting aside gratitude, which in any case must have made me her debtor for life, I loved her as affectionately as if she had been my sister: and at this moment, with seven-fold tenderness, from pity at witnessing her extreme dejection. I had, apparently, most reason for dejection, because I was leaving the saviour of my life: yet I, considering the shock my health had received, was cheerful and full of hope. She, on the contrary, who was parting with one who had had little means of serving her, except by kindness and brotherly treatment, was overcome by sorrow; so that, when I kissed her at our final farewell, she put her arms about my neck, and wept without speaking a word. I hoped to return in a week at farthest, and I agreed with her that on the fifth night from that, and every night afterwards, she should wait for me at six o'clock, near the bottom of Great Titchfield-street, which had been our customary haven, as it were, of rendezvous, to prevent our missing each other in the great Mediterranean of Oxford-street. This, and other measures of precaution I took: one only I forgot. She had either never told me, or (as a matter of no great interest) I had forgotten, her surname. It is a general practice, indeed, with girls of humble rank in her unhappy condition, not (as novel-reading women of higher pretensions) to style themselves—*Miss Douglass, Miss Montague,* &c. but simply by their Christian names, *Mary, Jane, Frances,* &c. Her surname, as the surest means of tracing her hereafter, I ought now to have inquired: but the truth is, having no reason to think that our meeting could, in consequence of a short interruption, be more difficult or uncertain than it had been for so many weeks, I had scarcely for a moment adverted to it as necessary, or placed it amongst my memoranda against this parting interview: and, my final anxieties being spent in comforting her with hopes, and in pressing upon her the necessity of getting some medicines for a violent cough and hoarseness with which she was troubled, I wholly forgot it until it was too late to recal her.

It was past eight o'clock when I reached the Gloucester Coffee-house: and, the Bristol Mail being on the point of going off, I mounted on the outside. The fine fluent motion* of this Mail soon laid me asleep: it is somewhat remarkable, that the first easy or refreshing sleep which I had enjoyed for some months, was on the outside of a Mail-coach—a bed which, at this day, I find rather an uneasy one. Connected with this sleep was a little incident, which served, as hundreds

---

* The Bristol Mail is the best appointed in the kingdom—owing to the double advantage of an unusually good road, and of an extra sum for expences subscribed by the Bristol merchants.

of others did at that time, to convince me how easily a man who has never been in any great distress, may pass through life without knowing, in his own person at least, anything of the possible goodness of the human heart—or, as I must add with a sigh, of its possible vileness. So thick a curtain of *manners* is drawn over the features and expression of men's *natures*, that to the ordinary observer, the two extremities, and the infinite field of varieties which lie between them, are all confounded—the vast and multitudinous compass of their several harmonies reduced to the meagre outline of differences expressed in the gamut or alphabet of elementary sounds. The case was this: for the first four or five miles from London, I annoyed my fellow passenger on the roof by occasionally falling against him when the coach gave a lurch to his side; and indeed, if the road had been less smooth and level than it is, I should have fallen off from weakness. Of this annoyance he complained heavily, as perhaps, in the same circumstances most people would; he expressed his complaint, however, more morosely than the occasion seemed to warrant; and, if I had parted with him at that moment, I should have thought of him (if I had considered it worth while to think of him at all) as a surly and almost brutal fellow. However, I was conscious that I had given him some cause for complaint: and, therefore, I apologized to him, and assured him I would do what I could to avoid falling asleep for the future; and, at the same time, in as few words as possible, I explained to him that I was ill and in a weak state from long suffering; and that I could not afford at that time to take an inside place. The man's manner changed, upon hearing this explanation, in an instant: and when I next woke for a minute from the noise and lights of Hounslow (for in spite of my wishes and efforts I had fallen asleep again within two minutes from the time I had spoken to him) I found that he had put his arm round me to protect me from falling off: and for the rest of my journey he behaved to me with the gentleness of a woman, so that, at length, I almost lay in his arms: and this was the more kind, as he could not have known that I was not going the whole way to Bath or Bristol. Unfortunately, indeed, I *did* go rather farther than I intended: for so genial and refreshing was my sleep, that the next time, after leaving Hounslow that I fully awoke, was upon the sudden pulling up of the Mail (possibly at a Post-office); and, on inquiry, I found that we had reached Maidenhead—six or seven miles, I think, a-head of Salt-hill. Here I alighted: and for the half minute that the Mail stopped, I was entreated by my friendly companion (who, from the transient glimpse I had had of him in Piccadilly, seemed to me to be a gentleman's butler—or person of that rank) to go to bed without delay. This I promised, though with no intention of doing so: and in fact, I immediately set forward, or rather backward, on foot. It must then have been nearly midnight: but so slowly did I creep along, that I heard a clock in a cottage strike four before I turned down the lane from Slough to Eton. The air and the sleep had both refreshed me; but I was weary nevertheless. I remember a thought (obvious enough, and which has been prettily expressed by a Roman poet) which gave me some consolation at that moment under my poverty. There had been some time before a murder committed on or near Hounslow-heath. I think I cannot be mistaken when I say that the name of the murdered person was *Steele*, and that he was the owner of a lavender plantation in that neighbourhood. Every step of my progress was bringing me nearer to the Heath: and it naturally occurred to me that I and the accursed murderer, if he were that night abroad, might at every instant be unconsciously approaching each other through the darkness: in which case, said I,—supposing I, instead of being (as indeed I am) little better than an outcast,—

> Lord of my learning and no land beside,

were, like my friend, Lord [Altamont], heir by general repute to 70,000*l*. per ann., what a panic should I be under at this moment about my throat!—indeed, it was not likely that Lord [Altamont] should ever be in my situation. But nevertheless, the spirit of the remark remains true—that vast power and possessions make a man shamefully afraid of dying: and I am convinced that many of the most intrepid adventurers, who, by fortunately being poor, enjoy the full use of their natural courage, would, if at the very instant of going into action news were brought to them that they had unexpectedly succeeded to an estate in England of 50,000*l*. a year, feel their dislike to bullets considerably sharpened*—and their efforts at perfect equanimity and self-possession proportionably difficult. So true it is, in the language of a wise man whose own experience had made him acquainted with both fortunes, that riches are better fitted—

> To slacken virtue, and abate her edge,
> Than tempt her to do ought may merit praise.
> *Parad. Regained.*

I dally with my subject because, to myself, the remembrance of these times is profoundly interesting. But my reader shall not have any further cause to complain: for I now hasten to its close.—In the road between Slough and Eton, I fell asleep: and, just as the morning began to dawn, I was awakened by the voice of a man standing over me and surveying me. I know not what he was: he was an ill-

---

*It will be objected that many men, of the highest rank and wealth, have in our own day, as well as throughout our history, been amongst the foremost in courting danger in battle. True: but this is not the case supposed; long familiarity with power has to them deadened its effect and its attractions.

looking fellow—but not therefore of necessity an ill-meaning fellow: or, if he were, I suppose he thought that no person sleeping out-of-doors in winter could be worth robbing. In which conclusion, however, as it regarded myself, I beg to assure him, if he should be among my readers, that he was mistaken. After a slight remark he passed on: and I was not sorry at his disturbance, as it enabled me to pass through Eton before people were generally up. The night had been heavy and lowering: but towards the morning it had changed to a slight frost: and the ground and the trees were now covered with rime. I slipped through Eton unobserved; washed myself, and, as far as possible, adjusted my dress at a little public-house in Windsor; and about eight o'clock went down towards Pote's. On my road I met some junior boys of whom I made inquiries: an Etonian is always a gentleman; and, in spite of my shabby habiliments, they answered me civilly. My friend, Lord [Altamont], was gone to the University of [Cambridge]. 'Ibi omnis effusus labor!' I had, however, other friends at Eton: but it is not to all who wear that name in prosperity that a man is willing to present himself in distress. On recollecting myself, however, I asked for the Earl of D[esart], to whom, (though my acquaintance with him was not so intimate as with some others) I should not have shrunk from presenting myself under any circumstances. He was still at Eton, though I believe on the wing for Cambridge. I called, was received kindly, and asked to breakfast.

Here let me stop for a moment to check my reader from any erroneous conclusions: because I have had occasion incidentally to speak of various patrician friends, it must not be supposed that I have myself any pretensions to rank or high blood. I thank God that I have not:—I am the son of a plain English merchant, esteemed during his life for his great integrity, and strongly attached to literary pursuits (indeed, he was himself, anonymously, an author): if he had lived, it was expected that he would have been very rich; but, dying prematurely, he left no more than about 30,000*l.* amongst seven different claimants. My mother I may mention with honour, as still more highly gifted. For, though unpretending to the name and honours of a *literary* woman, I shall presume to call her (what many literary women are not) an *intellectual* woman: and I believe that if ever her letters should be collected and published, they would be thought generally to exhibit as much strong and masculine sense, delivered in as pure 'mother English,' racy and fresh with idiomatic graces, as any in our language—hardly excepting those of lady M. W. Montague.—These are my honours of descent: I have no others: and I have thanked God sincerely that I have not, because, in my judgment, a station which raises a man too eminently above the level of his fellow-creatures is not the most favourable to moral, or to intellectual qualities.

27

Lord D[esart] placed before me a most magnificent breakfast. It was really so; but in my eyes it seemed trebly magnificent—from being the first regular meal, the first "good man's table," that I had sate down to for months. Strange to say, however, I could scarcely eat any thing. On the day when I first received my 10*l.* Bank-note, I had gone to a baker's shop and bought a couple of rolls: this very shop I had two months or six weeks before surveyed with an eagerness of desire which it was almost humiliating to me to recollect. I remembered the story about Otway; and feared that there might be danger in eating too rapidly. But I had no need for alarm, my appetite was quite sunk, and I became sick before I had eaten half of what I had bought. This effect from eating what approached to a meal, I continued to feel for weeks: or, when I did not experience any nausea, part of what I ate was rejected, sometimes with acidity, sometimes immediately, and without any acidity. On the present occasion, at Lord D[esart]'s table, I found myself not at all better than usual: and, in the midst of luxuries, I had no appetite. I had, however, unfortunately at all times a craving for wine: I explained my situation, therefore, to Lord D[esart], and gave him a short account of my late sufferings, at which he expressed great compassion, and called for wine. This gave me a momentary relief and pleasure; and on all occasions when I had an opportunity, I never failed to drink wine—which I worshipped then as I have since worshipped opium. I am convinced, however, that this indulgence in wine contributed to strengthen my malady; for the tone of my stomach was apparently quite sunk; and by a better regimen it might sooner, and perhaps effectually, have been revived. I hope that it was not from this love of wine that I lingered in the neighbourhood of my Eton friends: I persuaded myself *then* that it was from reluctance to ask of Lord D[esart], on whom I was conscious I had not sufficient claims, the particular service in quest of which I had come down to Eton. I was, however, unwilling to lose my journey, and—I asked it. Lord D[esart], whose good nature was unbounded, and which, in regard to myself, had been measured rather by his compassion perhaps for my condition, and his knowledge of my intimacy with some of his relatives, than by an over-rigorous inquiry into the extent of my own direct claims, faultered, nevertheless, at this request. He acknowledged that he did not like to have any dealings with money-lenders, and feared lest such a transaction might come to the ears of his connexions. Moreover, he doubted whether *his* signature, whose expectations were so much more bounded than those of [his cousin], would avail with my unchristian friends. However, he did not wish, as it seemed, to mortify me by an absolute refusal: for after a little consideration, he promised, under certain conditions which he pointed out, to give his security. Lord D[esart] was at this time not eighteen years of age: but I have often

28

doubted, on recollecting since the good sense and prudence which on this occasion he mingled with so much urbanity of manner (an urbanity which in him
wore the grace of youthful sincerity), whether any statesman—the oldest and the
most accomplished in diplomacy—could have acquitted himself better under the
same circumstances. Most people, indeed, cannot be addressed on such a business, without surveying you with looks as austere and unpropitious as those of a
Saracen's head.

Recomforted by this promise, which was not quite equal to the best, but far
above the worst that I had pictured to myself as possible, I returned in a Windsor
coach to London three days after I had quitted it. And now I come to the end of
my story:—the Jews did not approve of Lord D[esart]'s terms; whether they
would in the end have acceded to them, and were only seeking time for making
due inquiries, I know not; but many delays were made—time passed on—the
small fragment of my bank note had just melted away; and before any conclusion
could have been put to the business, I must have relapsed into my former state of
wretchedness. Suddenly, however, at this crisis, an opening was made, almost by
accident, for reconciliation with my friends. I quitted London, in haste, for a remote part of England: after some time, I proceeded to the university; and it was
not until many months had passed away, that I had it in my power again to re-
visit the ground which had become so interesting to me, and to this day remains
so, as the chief scene of my youthful sufferings.

Meantime, what had become of poor Anne? For her I have reserved my con-
cluding words: according to our agreement, I sought her daily, and waited for her
every night, so long as I staid in London, at the corner of Titchfield-street. I inquired for her of every one who was likely to know her; and, during the last hours
of my stay in London, I put into activity every means of tracing her that my
knowledge of London suggested, and the limited extent of my power made possible. The street where she had lodged I knew, but not the house; and I remembered at last some account which she had given me of ill treatment from her
landlord, which made it probable that she had quitted those lodgings before we
parted. She had few acquaintance; most people, besides, thought that the earnestness of my inquiries arose from motives which moved their laughter, or their
slight regard; and others, thinking I was in chase of a girl who had robbed me of
some trifles, were naturally and excusably indisposed to give me any clue to her,
if, indeed, they had any to give. Finally, as my despairing resource, on the day I
left London I put into the hands of the only person who (I was sure) must know
Anne by sight, from having been in company with us once or twice, an address
to [the Priory] in [Che]shire, at that time the residence of my family. But, to this

hour, I have never heard a syllable about her. This, amongst such troubles as most men meet with in this life, has been my heaviest affliction.—If she lived, doubtless we must have been sometimes in search of each other, at the very same moment, through the mighty labyrinths of London; perhaps, even within a few feet of each other—a barrier no wider in a London street, often amounting in the end to a separation for eternity! During some years, I hoped that she *did* live; and I suppose that, in the literal and unrhetorical use of the word *myriad,* I may say that on my different visits to London, I have looked into many, many myriads of female faces, in the hope of meeting her. I should know her again amongst a thousand, if I saw her for a moment; for, though not handsome, she had a sweet expression of countenance, and a peculiar and graceful carriage of the head.—I sought her, I have said, in hope. So it was for years; but now I should fear to see her; and her cough, which grieved me when I parted with her, is now my consolation. I now
wish to see her no longer; but think of her, more gladly, as one long since
laid in the grave; in the grave, I would hope, of a Magdalen;
taken away, before injuries and cruelty had blotted
out and transfigured her ingenuous nature,
or the brutalities of ruffians had
completed the ruin they
had begun.

CONFESSIONS OF AN ENGLISH OPIUM-EATER

Being an Extract from the Life of a Scholar

PART II

SO THEN, OXFORD-STREET, stony-hearted step-mother! thou that listenest to the sighs of orphans, and drinkest the tears of children, at length I was dismissed from thee: the time was come at last that I no more should pace in anguish thy never-ending terraces; no more should dream, and wake in captivity to the pangs of hunger. Successors, too many, to myself and Ann, have, doubtless, since then trodden in our footsteps—inheritors of our calamities: other orphans than Ann have sighed: tears have been shed by other children: and thou, Oxford-street, hast since, doubtless, echoed to the groans of innumerable hearts. For myself, however, the storm which I had outlived seemed to have been the pledge of a long fair-weather; the premature sufferings which I had paid down, to have been accepted as a ransom for many years to come, as a price of long immunity from sorrow: and if again I walked in London, a solitary and contemplative man (as oftentimes I did), I walked for the most part in serenity and peace of mind. And, although it is true that the calamities of my noviciate in London had struck root so deeply in my bodily constitution that afterwards they shot up and flourished afresh, and grew into a noxious umbrage that has overshadowed and darkened my latter years, yet these second assaults of suffering were met with a fortitude more confirmed, with the resources of a maturer intellect, and with alleviations from sympathising affection—how deep and tender!

Thus, however, with whatsoever alleviations, years that were far asunder were bound together by subtle links of suffering derived from a common root. And herein I notice an instance of the short-sightedness of human desires, that oftentimes on moonlight nights, during my first mournful abode in London, my consolation was (if such it could be thought) to gaze from Oxford-street up every avenue in succession which pierces through the heart of Marylebone to the fields and the woods; for *that*, said I, travelling with my eyes up the long vistas which lay part in light and part in shade, "*that* is the road to the North, and therefore to [Grasmere], and if I had the wings of a dove, *that* way I would fly for comfort." Thus I said, and thus I wished, in my blindness; yet, even in that very northern region it was, even in that very valley, nay, in that very house to which my erroneous wishes pointed, that this second birth of my sufferings began; and that they again threatened to besiege the citadel of life and hope. There it was, that for years I was persecuted by visions as ugly, and as ghastly phantoms as ever haunted the couch of an Orestes: and in this unhappier than he, that sleep, which comes to all as a respite and a restoration, and to him especially, as a blessed* balm for his wounded heart and his haunted brain, visited me as my bitterest scourge. Thus blind was I in my desires; yet, if a veil interposes between the dim-sightedness of man and his future calamities, the same veil hides from him their alleviations; and a grief which had not been feared is met by consolations which had not been hoped. I, therefore, who participated, as it were, in the troubles of Orestes (excepting only in his agitated conscience), participated no less in all his supports: my Eumenides, like his, were at my bed-feet, and stared in upon me through the curtains: but, watching by my pillow, or defrauding herself of sleep to bear me company through the heavy watches of the night, sate my Electra: for thou, beloved M[argaret], dear companion of my later years, thou wast my Electra! and neither in nobility of mind nor in long-suffering affection, wouldst permit that a Grecian sister should excel an English wife. For thou thoughtst not much to stoop to humble offices of kindness, and to servile† ministrations of tenderest affection;—to wipe away for years the unwholesome dews upon the forehead, or to refresh the lips when parched and baked with fever; nor, even when thy own peaceful slumbers had by long sympathy become infected with the spectacle of my dread contest with phantoms and shadowy enemies that oftentimes bade me "sleep no more!"—not even then, didst thou utter a complaint or any murmur, nor withdraw thy angelic smiles, nor shrink from thy service of love more than Electra did of old. For she too, though she was a Grecian woman, and the daughter of the king‡ of men, yet wept sometimes, and hid her face§ in her robe.

But these troubles are past: and thou wilt read these records of a period so dolorous to us both as the legend of some hideous dream that can return no more. Meantime, I am again in London: and again I pace the terraces of Oxford-

---

* Φίλον ὕπνου θέλγητρον ἐπίκουρον νόσου.

† ἡδὺ δούλευμα. EURIP. Orest.

‡ ἄναξ ἀνδρῶν Ἀγαμέμνων.

§ ὄμμα θεῖσ' εἴσω πέπλων. The scholar will know that throughout this passage I refer to the early scenes of the Orestes; one of the most beautiful exhibitions of the domestic affections which even the dramas of Euripides can furnish. To the Eng-lish reader, it may be necessary to say, that the situation at the opening of the drama is that of a brother attended only by his sister during the demoniacal possession of a suffering conscience (or, in the mythology of the play, haunted by the furies), and in circumstances of immediate danger from enemies, and of desertion or cold regard from nominal friends.

street by night: and oftentimes, when I am oppressed by anxieties that demand all my philosophy and the comfort of thy presence to support, and yet remember that I am separated from thee by three hundred miles, and the length of three dreary months,—I look up the streets that run northwards from Oxford-street, upon moonlight nights, and recollect my youthful ejaculation of anguish;—and remembering that thou art sitting alone in that same valley, and mistress of that very house to which my heart turned in its blindness nineteen years ago, I think that, though blind indeed, and scattered to the winds of late, the promptings of my heart may yet have had reference to a remoter time, and may be justified if read in another meaning:—and, if I could allow myself to descend again to the impotent wishes of childhood, I should again say to myself, as I look to the north, "Oh, that I had the wings of a dove—" and with how just a confidence in thy good and gracious nature might I add the other half of my early ejaculation—"And *that* way I would fly for comfort."

THE PLEASURES OF OPIUM

IT IS so long since I first took opium, that if it had been a trifling incident in my life, I might have forgotten its date: but cardinal events are not to be forgotten; and from circumstances connected with it, I remember that it must be referred to the autumn of 1804. During that season I was in London, having come thither for the first time since my entrance at college. And my introduction to opium arose in the following way. From an early age I had been accustomed to wash my head in cold water at least once a day: being suddenly seized with toothache, I attributed it to some relaxation caused by an accidental intermission of that practice; jumped out of bed; plunged my head into a bason of cold water; and with hair thus wetted went to sleep. The next morning, as I need hardly say, I awoke with excruciating rheumatic pains of the head and face, from which I had hardly any respite for about twenty days. On the twenty-first day, I think it was, and on a Sunday, that I went out into the streets; rather to run away, if possible, from my torments, than with any distinct purpose. By accident I met a college acquaintance who recommended opium. Opium! dread agent of unimaginable pleasure and pain! I had heard of it as I had of manna or of Ambrosia, but no further: how unmeaning a sound was it at that time! what solemn chords does it now strike upon my heart! what heart-quaking vibrations of sad and happy remembrances! Reverting for a moment to these, I feel a mystic importance attached to the minutest circumstances connected with the place and the time, and the man (if man he was) that first laid open to me the Paradise of Opium-eaters. It was a Sunday afternoon, wet and cheerless: and a duller spectacle this earth of ours has not to show than a rainy Sunday in London. My road homewards lay through Oxford-street; and near "the *stately* Pantheon," (as Mr. Wordsworth has obligingly called it) I saw a druggist's shop. The druggist—unconscious minister of celestial pleasures!—as if in sympathy with the rainy Sunday, looked dull and stupid, just as any mortal druggist might be expected to look on a Sunday; and, when I asked for the tincture of opium, he gave it to me as any other man might do: and furthermore, out of my shilling, returned me what seemed to be real copper halfpence, taken out of a real wooden drawer. Nevertheless, in spite of such indications of humanity, he has ever since existed in my mind as the beatific vision of an immortal druggist, sent down to earth on a special mission to myself. And it confirms me in this way of considering him, that, when I next came up to London, I sought him near the stately Pantheon, and found him not: and thus to me, who knew not his name (if indeed he had one) he seemed rather to have vanished from Oxford-street than to have removed in any bodily fashion. The reader may choose to think of him as, possibly, no more than a sublunary druggist: it may be so: but my faith is better: I believe him to have evanesced,* or evaporated. So unwillingly would I connect any mortal remembrances with that hour, and place, and creature, that first brought me acquainted with the celestial drug.

Arrived at my lodgings, it may be supposed that I lost not a moment in taking the quantity prescribed. I was necessarily ignorant of the whole art and mystery of opium-taking: and, what I took, I took under every disadvantage. But I took it:—and in an hour, oh! Heavens! what a revulsion! what an upheaving, from its lowest depths, of the inner spirit! what an apocalypse of the world within me! That my pains had vanished, was now a trifle in my eyes:—this negative effect was swallowed up in the immensity of those positive effects which had opened before me—in the abyss of divine enjoyment thus suddenly revealed. Here was a panacea —a φάρμακον νηπενθές for all human woes: here was the secret of happiness, about which philosophers had disputed for so many ages, at once discovered: happiness might now be bought for a penny, and carried in the waistcoat pocket: portable ecstasies might be had corked up in a pint bottle: and peace of mind could be sent down in gallons by the mail coach. But, if I talk in this way, the reader will think I am laughing: and I can assure him, that nobody will laugh long who deals much with opium: its pleasures even are of a grave and solemn complexion; and in his happiest state, the opium-eater cannot present himself in the character of *l'Allegro*: even then, he speaks and thinks as becomes *Il Penseroso*. Nevertheless, I have a very reprehensible way of jesting at times in the midst of my own misery: and, unless when I am checked by some more powerful feelings, I am afraid I shall be guilty of this indecent practice even in these annals of suffering or enjoyment. The reader must allow a little to my infirm nature in this respect: and with a few indulgences of that sort, I shall endeavour to be as grave, if not drowsy, as fits a theme like opium, so anti-mercurial as it really is, and so drowsy as it is falsely reputed.

And, first, one word with respect to its bodily effects: for upon all that has been hitherto written on the subject of opium, whether by travellers in Turkey

---

* *Evanesced:*—this way of going off the stage of life appears to have been well known in the 17th century, but at that time to have been considered a peculiar privilege of blood-royal, and by no means to be allowed to druggists. For about the year 1686, a poet of rather ominous name (and who, by the bye, did ample justice to his name), viz. Mr. *Flat-man*, in speaking of the death of Charles II. expresses his surprise that any prince should commit so absurd an act as dying; because, says he,

Kings should disdain to die, and only *disappear*.
They should *abscond*, that is, into the other world.

(who may plead their privilege of lying as an old immemorial right), or by professors of medicine, writing *ex cathedra*,—I have but one emphatic criticism to pronounce—Lies! lies! lies! I remember once, in passing a book-stall, to have caught these words from a page of some satiric author:—"By this time I became convinced that the London newspapers spoke truth at least twice a week, viz. on Tuesday and Saturday, and might safely be depended upon for——the list of bankrupts." In like manner, I do by no means deny that some truths have been delivered to the world in regard to opium: thus it has been repeatedly affirmed by the learned, that opium is a dusky brown in colour; and this, take notice, I grant: secondly, that it is rather dear; which also I grant: for in my time, East-India opium has been three guineas a pound, and Turkey eight: and, thirdly, that if you eat a good deal of it, most probably you must——do what is particularly disagreeable to any man of regular habits, viz. die.* These weighty propositions are, all and singular, true: I cannot gainsay them: and truth ever was, and will be, commendable. But in these three theorems, I believe we have exhausted the stock of knowledge as yet accumulated by man on the subject of opium. And therefore, worthy doctors, as there seems to be room for further discoveries, stand aside, and allow me to come forward and lecture on this matter.

First, then, it is not so much affirmed as taken for granted, by all who ever mention opium, formally or incidentally, that it does, or can, produce intoxication. Now, reader, assure yourself, *meo periculo*, that no quantity of opium ever did, or could intoxicate. As to the tincture of opium (commonly called laudanum) *that* might certainly intoxicate if a man could bear to take enough of it; but why? because it contains so much proof spirit, and not because it contains so much opium. But crude opium, I affirm peremptorily, is incapable of producing any state of body at all resembling that which is produced by alcohol; and not in *degree* only incapable, but even in *kind*: it is not in the quantity of its effects merely, but in the quality, that it differs altogether. The pleasure given by wine is always mounting, and tending to a crisis, after which it declines: that from opium, when once generated, is stationary for eight or ten hours: the first, to borrow a technical distinction from medicine, is a case of acute—the second, of chronic pleasure: the one is a flame, the other a steady and equable glow. But the main distinction lies in this, that whereas wine disorders the mental faculties, opium, on the contrary (if taken in a proper manner), introduces amongst them

* Of this, however, the learned appear latterly to have doubted: for in a pirated edition of Buchan's *Domestic Medicine*, which I once saw in the hands of a farmer's wife who was studying it for the benefit of her health, the Doctor was made to say—"Be particularly careful never to take above five-and-twenty *ounces* of laudanum at once;" the true reading being probably five-and-twenty *drops*, which are held equal to about one grain of crude opium.

36

the most exquisite order, legislation, and harmony. Wine robs a man of his self-possession: opium greatly invigorates it. Wine unsettles and clouds the judgment, and gives a preternatural brightness, and a vivid exaltation to the contempts and the admirations, the loves and the hatreds, of the drinker: opium, on the contrary, communicates serenity and equipoise to all the faculties, active or passive: and with respect to the temper and moral feelings in general, it gives simply that sort of vital warmth which is approved by the judgment, and which would probably always accompany a bodily constitution of primeval or antediluvian health. Thus, for instance, opium, like wine, gives an expansion to the heart and the benevolent affections: but then, with this remarkable difference, that in the sudden developement of kind-heartedness which accompanies inebriation, there is always more or less of a maudlin character, which exposes it to the contempt of the by-stander. Men shake hands, swear eternal friendship, and shed tears—no mortal knows why: and the sensual creature is clearly uppermost. But the expansion of the benigner feelings, incident to opium, is no febrile access, but a healthy restoration to that state which the mind would naturally recover upon the removal of any deep-seated irritation of pain that had disturbed and quarrelled with the impulses of a heart originally just and good. True it is, that even wine, up to a certain point, and with certain men, rather tends to exalt and to steady the intellect: I myself, who have never been a great wine-drinker, used to find that half a dozen glasses of wine advantageously affected the faculties—brightened and intensified the consciousness—and gave to the mind a feeling of being "ponderibus librata suis:" and certainly it is most absurdly said, in popular language, of any man, that he is *disguised* in liquor: for, on the contrary, most men are disguised by sobriety; and it is when they are drinking (as some old gentleman says in Athenæus), that men ἑαυτοὺς ἐμφανίζουσιν οἵτινές εἰσιν. —display themselves in their true complexion of character; which surely is not disguising themselves. But still, wine constantly leads a man to the brink of absurdity and extravagance; and, beyond a certain point, it is sure to volatilize and to disperse the intellectual energies: whereas opium always seems to compose what had been agitated, and to concentrate what had been distracted. In short, to sum up all in one word, a man who is inebriated, or tending to inebriation, is, and feels that he is, in a condition which calls up into supremacy the merely human, too often the brutal, part of his nature: but the opium-eater (I speak of him who is not suffering from any disease, or other remote effects of opium) feels that the diviner part of his nature is paramount; that is, the moral affections are in a state of cloudless serenity; and over all is the great light of the majestic intellect.

This is the doctrine of the true church on the subject of opium: of which

37

church I acknowledge myself to be the only member—the alpha and the omega: but then it is to be recollected, that I speak from the ground of a large and profound personal experience: whereas most of the unscientific* authors who have at all treated of opium, and even of those who have written expressly on the materia medica, make it evident, from the horror they express of it, that their experimental knowledge of its action is none at all. I will, however, candidly acknowledge that I have met with one person who bore evidence to its intoxicating power, such as staggered my own incredulity: for he was a surgeon, and had himself taken opium largely. I happened to say to him, that his enemies (as I had heard) charged him with talking nonsense on politics, and that his friends apologized for him, by suggesting that he was constantly in a state of intoxication from opium. Now the accusation, said I, is not *primâ facie*, and of necessity, an absurd one: but the defence *is*. To my surprise, however, he insisted that both his enemies and his friends were in the right: "I will maintain," said he, "that I *do* talk nonsense; and secondly, I will maintain that I do not talk nonsense upon principle, or with any view to profit, but solely and simply, said he, solely and simply,—solely and simply (repeating it three times over), because I am drunk with opium; and *that* daily." I replied that, as to the allegation of his enemies, as it seemed to be established upon such respectable testimony, seeing that the three parties concerned all agreed in it, it did not become me to question it; but the defence set up I must demur to. He proceeded to discuss the matter, and to lay down his reasons: but it seemed to me so impolite to pursue an argument which must have presumed a man mistaken in a point belonging to his own profession, that I did not press him even when his course of argument seemed open to objection: not to mention that a man who talks nonsense, even though "with no

* Amongst the great herd of travellers, &c. who show sufficiently by their stupidity that they never held any intercourse with opium, I must caution my readers specially against the brilliant author of "*Anastasius*." This gentleman, whose wit would lead one to presume him an opium-eater, has made it impossible to consider him in that character from the grievous misrepresentation which he gives of its effects, at pp. 215-17, of vol. 1.—Upon consideration it must appear such to the author himself: for, waiving the errors I have insisted on in the text, which (and others) are adopted in the fullest manner, he will himself admit, that an old gentleman "with a snow-white beard," who eats "ample doses of opium," and is yet able to deliver what is meant and received as very weighty counsel on the bad effects of that practice, is but an indifferent evidence that opium either kills people prematurely, or sends them into a madhouse. But, for my part, I see into this old gentleman and his motives: the fact is, he was enamoured of "the little golden receptacle of the pernicious drug" which Anastasius carried about him; and no way of obtaining it so safe and so feasible occurred, as that of frightening its owner out of his wits (which, by the bye, are none of the strongest). This commentary throws a new light upon the case, and greatly improves it as a story: for the old gentleman's speech, considered as a lecture on pharmacy, is highly absurd: but, considered as a hoax on Anastasius, it reads excellently.

view to profit," is not altogether the most agreeable partner in a dispute, whether as opponent or respondent. I confess, however, that the authority of a surgeon, and one who was reputed a good one, may seem a weighty one to my prejudice: but still I must plead my experience, which was greater than his greatest by 7000 drops a day; and, though it was not possible to suppose a medical man unacquainted with the characteristic symptoms of vinous intoxication, it yet struck me that he might proceed on a logical error of using the word intoxication with too great latitude, and extending it generically to all modes of nervous excitement, instead of restricting it as the expression for a specific sort of excitement, connected with certain diagnostics. Some people have maintained, in my hearing, that they had been drunk upon green tea: and a medical student in London, for whose knowledge in his profession I have reason to feel great respect, assured me, the other day, that a patient, in recovering from an illness, had got drunk on a beef-steak.

Having dwelt so much on this first and leading error, in respect to opium, I shall notice very briefly a second and a third; which are, that the elevation of spirits produced by opium is necessarily followed by a proportionate depression, and that the natural and even immediate consequence of opium is torpor and stagnation, animal and mental. The first of these errors I shall content myself with simply denying; assuring my reader, that for ten years, during which I took opium at intervals, the day succeeding to that on which I allowed myself this luxury was always a day of unusually good spirits.

With respect to the torpor supposed to follow, or rather (if we were to credit the numerous pictures of Turkish opium-eaters) to accompany the practice of opium-eating, I deny that also. Certainly, opium is classed under the head of narcotics; and some such effect it may produce in the end: but the primary effects of opium are always, and in the highest degree, to excite and stimulate the system: this first stage of its action always lasted with me, during my noviciate, for upwards of eight hours; so that it must be the fault of the opium-eater himself if he does not so time his exhibition of the dose (to speak medically) as that the whole weight of its narcotic influence may descend upon his sleep. Turkish opium-eaters, it seems, are absurd enough to sit, like so many equestrian statues, on logs of wood as stupid as themselves. But that the reader may judge of the degree in which opium is likely to stupify the faculties of an Englishman, I shall (by way of treating the question illustratively, rather than argumentatively) describe the way in which I myself often passed an opium evening in London, during the period between 1804—1812. It will be seen, that at least opium did not move me to seek solitude, and much less to seek inactivity, or the torpid state of self-involution ascribed to the Turks. I give this account at the risk of being pronounced a crazy enthusiast or visionary: but I regard *that* little: I must desire my reader to bear in mind, that I was a hard student, and at severe studies for all the rest of my time: and certainly I had a right occasionally to relaxations as well as other people: these, however, I allowed myself but seldom.

The late Duke of [Norfolk] used to say, "Next Friday, by the blessing of Heaven, I purpose to be drunk:" and in like manner I used to fix beforehand how often, within a given time, and when, I would commit a debauch of opium. This was seldom more than once in three weeks: for at that time I could not have ventured to call every day (as I did afterwards) for *"a glass of laudanum negus, warm, and without sugar."* No: as I have said, I seldom drank laudanum, at that time, more than once in three weeks: this was usually on a Tuesday or a Saturday night; my reason for which was this. In those days Grassini sang at the Opera: and her voice was delightful to me beyond all that I had ever heard. I know not what may be the state of the Opera-house now, having never been within its walls for seven or eight years, but at that time it was by much the most pleasant place of public resort in London for passing an evening. Five shillings admitted one to the gallery, which was subject to far less annoyance than the pit of the theatres: the orchestra was distinguished by its sweet and melodious grandeur from all English orchestras, the composition of which, I confess, is not acceptable to my ear, from the predominance of the clangorous instruments, and the absolute tyranny of the violin. The choruses were divine to hear: and when Grassini appeared in some interlude, as she often did, and poured forth her passionate soul as Andromache, at the tomb of Hector, &c. I question whether any Turk, of all that ever entered the Paradise of opium-eaters, can have had half the pleasure I had. But, indeed, I honour the Barbarians too much by supposing them capable of any pleasures approaching to the intellectual ones of an Englishman. For music is an intellectual or a sensual pleasure, according to the temperament of him who hears it. And, by the bye, with the exception of the fine extravaganza on that subject in Twelfth Night, I do not recollect more than one thing said adequately on the subject of music in all literature: it is a passage in the *Religio Medici** of Sir T. Brown; and, though chiefly remarkable for its sublimity, has also a philosophic value, inasmuch as it points to the true theory of musical effects. The mistake of most people is to suppose that it is by the ear they communicate with music, and, therefore, that they are purely passive to its effects. But this is not so: it is by the re-action of the mind upon the notices of the ear,

---

*I have not the book at this moment to consult: but I think the passage begins—"And even that tavern music, which makes one man merry, another mad, in me strikes a deep fit of devotion," &c.

(the *matter* coming by the senses, the *form* from the mind) that the pleasure is constructed: and therefore it is that people of equally good ear differ so much in this point from one another. Now opium, by greatly increasing the activity of the mind generally, increases, of necessity, that particular mode of its activity by which we are able to construct out of the raw material of organic sound an elaborate intellectual pleasure. But, says a friend, a succession of musical sounds is to me like a collection of Arabic characters: I can attach no ideas to them. Ideas! my good sir? there is no occasion for them: all that class of ideas, which can be available in such a case, has a language of representative feelings. But this is a subject foreign to my present purposes: it is sufficient to say, that a chorus, &c. of elaborate harmony, displayed before me, as in a piece of arras work, the whole of my past life—not, as if recalled by an act of memory, but as if present and incarnated in the music: no longer painful to dwell upon: but the detail of its incidents removed, or blended in some hazy abstraction; and its passions exalted, spiritualized, and sublimed. All this was to be had for five shillings. And over and above the music of the stage and the orchestra, I had all around me, in the intervals of the performance, the music of the Italian language talked by Italian women: for the gallery was usually crowded with Italians: and I listened with a pleasure such as that with which Weld the traveller lay and listened, in Canada, to the sweet laughter of Indian women; for the less you understand of a language, the more sensible you are to the melody or harshness of its sounds: for such a purpose, therefore, it was an advantage to me that I was a poor Italian scholar, reading it but little, and not speaking it at all, nor understanding a tenth part of what I heard spoken.

These were my Opera pleasures: but another pleasure I had which, as it could be had only on a Saturday night, occasionally struggled with my love of the Opera; for, at that time, Tuesday and Saturday were the regular Opera nights. On this subject I am afraid I shall be rather obscure, but, I can assure the reader, not at all more so than Marinus in his life of Proclus, or many other biographers and auto-biographers of fair reputation. This pleasure, I have said, was to be had only on a Saturday night. What then was Saturday night to me more than any other night? I had no labours that I rested from; no wages to receive: what needed I to care for Saturday night, more than as it was a summons to hear Grassini? True, most logical reader: what you say is unanswerable. And yet so it was and is, that, whereas different men throw their feelings into different channels, and most are apt to show their interest in the concerns of the poor, chiefly by sympathy, expressed in some shape or other, with their distresses and sorrows, I, at that time, was disposed to express my interest by sympathising with their plea-

41

sures. The pains of poverty I had lately seen too much of; more than I wished to remember: but the pleasures of the poor, their consolations of spirit, and their reposes from bodily toil, can never become oppressive to contemplate. Now Saturday night is the season for the chief, regular, and periodic return of rest to the poor: in this point the most hostile sects unite, and acknowledge a common link of brotherhood: almost all Christendom rests from its labours. It is a rest introductory to another rest: and divided by a whole day and two nights from the renewal of toil. On this account I feel always, on a Saturday night, as though I also were released from some yoke of labour, had some wages to receive, and some luxury of repose to enjoy. For the sake, therefore, of witnessing, upon as large a scale as possible, a spectacle with which my sympathy was so entire, I used often, on Saturday nights, after I had taken opium, to wander forth, without much regarding the direction or the distance, to all the markets, and other parts of London, to which the poor resort on a Saturday night, for laying out their wages. Many a family party, consisting of a man, his wife, and sometimes one or two of his children, have I listened to, as they stood consulting on their ways and means, or the strength of their exchequer, or the price of household articles. Gradually I became familiar with their wishes, their difficulties, and their opinions. Sometimes there might be heard murmurs of discontent: but far oftener expressions on the countenance, or uttered in words, of patience, hope, and tranquillity. And taken generally, I must say, that, in this point at least, the poor are far more philosophic than the rich—that they show a more ready and cheerful submission to what they consider as irremediable evils, or irreparable losses. Whenever I saw occasion, or could do it without appearing to be intrusive, I joined their parties; and gave my opinion upon the matter in discussion, which, if not always judicious, was always received indulgently. If wages were a little higher, or expected to be so, or the quartern loaf a little lower, or it was reported that onions and butter were expected to fall, I was glad: yet, if the contrary were true, I drew from opium some means of consoling myself. For opium (like the bee, that extracts its materials indiscriminately from roses and from the soot of chimneys) can overrule all feelings into a compliance with the master key. Some of these rambles led me to great distances: for an opium-eater is too happy to observe the motion of time. And sometimes in my attempts to steer homewards, upon nautical principles, by fixing my eye on the pole-star, and seeking ambitiously for a north-west passage, instead of circumnavigating all the capes and head-lands I had doubled in my outward voyage, I came suddenly upon such knotty problems of alleys, such enigmatical entries, and such sphynx's riddles of streets without thoroughfares, as must, I conceive, baffle the audacity of porters, and confound the intellects of hackney-coachmen. I could almost have believed, at times, that I must be the first discoverer of some of these *terræ incognitæ*, and doubted, whether they had yet been laid down in the modern charts of London. For all this, however, I paid a heavy price in distant years, when the human face tyrannized over my dreams, and the perplexities of my steps in London came back and haunted my sleep, with the feeling of perplexities moral or intellectual, that brought confusion to the reason, or anguish and remorse to the conscience.

Thus I have shown that opium does not, of necessity, produce inactivity or torpor; but that, on the contrary, it often led me into markets and theatres. Yet, in candour, I will admit that markets and theatres are not the appropriate haunts of the opium-eater, when in the divinest state incident to his enjoyment. In that state, crowds become an oppression to him; music even, too sensual and gross. He naturally seeks solitude and silence, as indispensable conditions of those trances, or profoundest reveries, which are the crown and consummation of what opium can do for human nature. I, whose disease it was to meditate too much, and to observe too little, and who, upon my first entrance at college, was nearly falling into a deep melancholy, from brooding too much on the sufferings which I had witnessed in London, was sufficiently aware of the tendencies of my own thoughts to do all I could to counteract them.—I was, indeed, like a person who, according to the old legend, had entered the cave of Trophonius: and the remedies I sought were to force myself into society, and to keep my understanding in continual activity upon matters of science. But for these remedies, I should certainly have become hypochondriacally melancholy. In after years, however, when my cheerfulness was more fully re-established, I yielded to my natural inclination for a solitary life. And, at that time, I often fell into these reveries upon taking opium; and more than once it has happened to me, on a summer-night, when I have been at an open window, in a room from which I could overlook the sea at a mile below me, and could command a view of the great town of L[iverpool], at about the same distance, that I have sate, from sun-set to sun-rise, motionless, and without wishing to move.

I shall be charged with mysticism, Behmenism, quietism, &c. but *that* shall not alarm me. Sir H. Vane, the younger, was one of our wisest men: and let my readers see if he, in his philosophical works, be half as unmystical as I am.—I say, then, that it has often struck me that the scene itself was somewhat typical of what took place in such a reverie. The town of L[iverpool] represented the earth, with its sorrows and its graves left behind, yet not out of sight, nor wholly forgotten. The ocean, in everlasting but gentle agitation, and brooded over by a dove-like calm, might not unfitly typify the mind and the mood which then

43

swayed it. For it seemed to me as if then first I stood at a distance, and aloof from the uproar of life; as if the tumult, the fever, and the strife, were suspended; a respite granted from the secret burthens of the heart; a sabbath of repose; a resting from human labours. Here were the hopes which blossom in the paths of life, reconciled with the peace which is in the grave; motions of the intellect as unwearied as the heavens, yet for all anxieties a halcyon calm: a tranquillity that seemed no product of inertia, but as if resulting from mighty and equal antagonisms; infinite activities, infinite repose.

Oh! just, subtle, and mighty opium! that to the hearts of poor and rich alike, for the wounds that will never heal, and for "the pangs that tempt the spirit to rebel," bringest an assuaging balm; eloquent opium! that with thy potent rhetoric stealest away the purposes of wrath; and to the guilty man, for one night givest back the hopes of his youth, and hands washed pure from blood; and to the proud man, a brief oblivion for

Wrongs unredress'd, and insults unavenged;

that summonest to the chancery of dreams, for the triumphs of suffering innocence, false witnesses; and confoundest perjury; and dost reverse the sentences of unrighteous judges:—thou buildest upon the bosom of darkness, out of the fantastic imagery of the brain, cities and temples, beyond the art of Phidias and Praxiteles—beyond the splendour of Babylon and Hekatómpylos: and "from the anarchy of dreaming sleep," callest into sunny light the faces of long-buried beauties, and the blessed household countenances, cleansed from the "dishonours of the grave." Thou only givest these gifts to man; and thou hast the keys of Paradise, oh, just, subtle, and mighty opium!

INTRODUCTION TO THE
PAINS OF OPIUM

COURTEOUS, and, I hope, indulgent reader (for all *my* readers must be indulgent ones, or else, I fear, I shall shock them too much to count on their courtesy), having accompanied me thus far, now let me request you to move onwards, for about eight years; that is to say, from 1804 (when I have said that my acquaintance with opium first began) to 1812. The years of academic life are now over and gone—almost forgotten:—the student's cap no longer presses my temples; if my cap exist at all, it presses those of some youthful scholar, I trust, as happy as myself, and as passionate a lover of knowledge. My gown is, by this time, I dare to say, in the same condition with many thousands of excellent books in the Bodleian, viz. diligently perused by certain studious moths and worms: or departed, however (which is all that I know of its fate), to that great reservoir of *somewhere*, to which all the tea-cups, tea-caddies, tea-pots, tea-kettles, &c. have departed (not to speak of still frailer vessels, such as glasses, decanters, bed-makers, &c.) which occasional resemblances in the present generation of tea-cups, &c. remind me of having once possessed, but of whose departure and final fate I, in common with most gownsmen of either university, could give, I suspect, but an obscure and conjectural history. The persecutions of the chapel-bell, sounding its unwelcome summons to six o'clock matins, interrupts my slumbers no longer: the porter who rang it, upon whose beautiful nose (bronze, inlaid with copper) I wrote, in retaliation, so many Greek epigrams, whilst I was dressing, is dead, and has ceased to disturb any body: and I, and many others, who suffered much from his tintinnabulous propensities, have now agreed to overlook his errors, and have forgiven him. Even with the bell I am now in charity: it rings, I suppose, as formerly, thrice a-day: and cruelly annoys, I doubt not, many worthy gentlemen, and disturbs their peace of mind: but as to me, in this year 1812, I regard its treacherous voice no longer (treacherous, I call it, for, by some refinement of malice, it spoke in as sweet and silvery tones as if it had been inviting one to a party): its tones have no longer, indeed, power to reach me, let the wind sit as favourable as the malice of the bell itself could wish: for I am 250 miles away from it, and buried in the depth of mountains. And what am I doing amongst the mountains? Taking opium. Yes, but what else? Why, reader, in 1812, the year we are now arrived at, as well as for some years previous, I have been chiefly studying German metaphysics, in the writings of Kant, Fichte,

Schelling, &c. And how, and in what manner, do I live? in short, what class or description of men do I belong to? I am at this period, viz. in 1812, living in a cottage; and with a single female servant (honi soit qui mal y pense), who, amongst my neighbours, passes by the name of my "house-keeper." And, as a scholar and a man of learned education, and in that sense a gentleman, I may presume to class myself as an unworthy member of that indefinite body called *gentlemen*. Partly on the ground I have assigned, perhaps; partly because, from my having no visible calling or business, it is rightly judged that I must be living on my private fortune; I am so classed by my neighbours: and, by the courtesy of modern England, I am usually addressed on letters, &c. *esquire*, though having, I fear, in the rigorous construction of heralds, but slender pretensions to that distinguished honour: yes, in popular estimation, I am X. Y. Z., esquire, but not Justice of the Peace, nor Custos Rotulorum. Am I married? Not yet. And I still take opium? On Saturday nights. And, perhaps, have taken it unblushingly ever since "the rainy Sunday," and "the stately Pantheon," and "the beatific druggist" of 1804?—Even so. And how do I find my health after all this opium-eating? in short, how do I do? Why, pretty well, I thank you, reader: in the phrase of ladies in the straw, "as well as can be expected." In fact, if I dared to say the real and simple truth, though, to satisfy the theories of medical men, I *ought* to be ill, I never was better in my life than in the spring of 1812; and I hope sincerely, that the quantity of claret, port, or "particular Madeira," which, in all probability, you, good reader, have taken, and design to take, for every term of eight years, during your natural life, may as little disorder your health as mine was disordered by the opium I had taken for the eight years, between 1804 & 1812. Hence you may see again the danger of taking any medical advice from *Anastasius*; in divinity, for aught I know, or law, he may be a safe counsellor; but not in medicine. No: it is far better to consult Dr. Buchan; as I did: for I never forgot that worthy man's excellent suggestion: and I was "particularly careful not to take above five-and-twenty ounces of laudanum." To this moderation and temperate use of the article, I may ascribe it, I suppose, that as yet, at least, (*i.e.* in 1812,) I am ignorant and unsuspicious of the avenging terrors which opium has in store for those who abuse its lenity. At the same time, it must not be forgotten, that hitherto I have been only a dilettante eater of opium: eight years' practice even, with the single precaution of allowing sufficient intervals between every indulgence, has not been sufficient to make opium necessary to me as an article of daily diet. But now comes a different era. Move on, if you please, reader, to 1813. In the summer of the year we have just quitted, I had suffered much in bodily health from distress of mind connected with a very melancholy event. This

46

event, being no ways related to the subject now before me, further than through the bodily illness which it produced, I need not more particularly notice. Whether this illness of 1812 had any share in that of 1813, I know not: but so it was, that in the latter year, I was attacked by a most appalling irritation of the stomach, in all respects the same as that which had caused me so much suffering in youth, and accompanied by a revival of all the old dreams. This is the point of my narrative on which, as respects my own self-justification, the whole of what follows may be said to hinge. And here I find myself in a perplexing dilemma:—Either, on the one hand, I must exhaust the reader's patience, by such a detail of my malady, or of my struggles with it, as might suffice to establish the fact of my inability to wrestle any longer with irritation and constant suffering: or, on the other hand, by passing lightly over this critical part of my story, I must forego the benefit of a stronger impression left on the mind of the reader, and must lay myself open to the misconstruction of having slipped by the easy and gradual steps of self-indulging persons, from the first to the final stage of opium-eating (a misconstruction to which there will be a lurking predisposition in most readers, from my previous acknowledgments.) This is the dilemma: the first horn of which would be sufficient to toss and gore any column of patient readers, though drawn up sixteen deep and constantly relieved by fresh men: consequently *that* is not to be thought of. It remains then, that I *postulate* so much as is necessary for my purpose. And let me take as full credit for what I postulate as if I had demonstrated it, good reader, at the expense of your patience and my own. Be not so ungenerous as to let me suffer in your good opinion through my own forbearance and regard for your comfort. No: believe all that I ask of you, viz. that I could resist no longer, believe it liberally, and as an act of grace: or else in mere prudence: for, if not, then in the next edition of my Opium Confessions revised and enlarged, I will make you believe and tremble: and *à force d'ennuyer*, by mere dint of pandiculation I will terrify all readers of mine from ever again questioning any postulate that I shall think fit to make.

This then, let me repeat, I postulate—that, at the time I began to take opium daily, I could not have done otherwise. Whether, indeed, afterwards I might not have succeeded in breaking off the habit, even when it seemed to me that all efforts would be unavailing, and whether many of the innumerable efforts which I *did* make, might not have been carried much further, and my gradual reconquests of ground lost might not have been followed up much more energetically—these are questions which I must decline. Perhaps I might make out a case of palliation; but, shall I speak ingenuously? I confess it, as a besetting infirmity of mine, that I am too much of an Eudæmonist: I hanker too much after a state of happiness, both for myself and others: I cannot face misery, whether my own or not, with an eye of sufficient firmness: and am little capable of encountering present pain for the sake of any reversionary benefit. On some other matters, I can agree with the gentlemen in the cotton-trade* at Manchester in affecting the Stoic philosophy: but not in this. Here I take the liberty of an Eclectic philosopher, and I look out for some courteous and considerate sect that will condescend more to the infirm condition of an opium-eater; that are 'sweet men,' as Chaucer says, 'to give absolution,' and will show some conscience in the penances they inflict, and the efforts of abstinence they exact, from poor sinners like myself. An in-human moralist I can no more endure in my nervous state than opium that has not been boiled. At any rate, he, who summons me to send out a large freight of self-denial and mortification upon any cruising voyage of moral improvement, must make it clear to my understanding that the concern is a hopeful one. At my time of life (six and thirty years of age) it cannot be supposed that I have much energy to spare: in fact, I find it all little enough for the intellectual labours I have on my hands: and, therefore, let no man expect to frighten me by a few hard words into embarking any part of it upon desperate adventures of morality.

Whether desperate or not, however, the issue of the struggle in 1813 was what I have mentioned; and from this date, the reader is to consider me as a regular and confirmed opium-eater, of whom to ask whether on any particular day he had or had not taken opium, would be to ask whether his lungs had performed respiration, or the heart fulfilled its functions.—You understand now, reader, what I am: and you are by this time aware, that no old gentleman, "with a snow-white beard," will have any chance of persuading me to surrender "the little golden receptacle of the pernicious drug." No: I give notice to all, whether moral-ists or surgeons, that, whatever be their pretensions and skill in their respective lines of practice, they must not hope for any countenance from me, if they think to begin by any savage proposition for a Lent or Ramadan of abstinence from opium. This then being all fully understood between us, we shall in future sail before the wind. Now then, reader, from 1813, where all this time we have been sitting down and loitering—rise up, if you please, and walk forward about three years more. Now draw up the curtain, and you shall see me in a new character.

If any man, poor or rich, were to say that he would tell us what had been the happiest day in his life, and the why, and the wherefore, I suppose that we should

---

* A handsome news-room, of which I was very politely made free in passing through Manchester by several gentlemen of that place, is called, I think, *The Porch:* whence I, who am a stranger in Manchester, inferred that the subscribers meant to profess themselves followers of Zeno. But I have been since assured that this is a mistake.

all cry out—Hear him! Hear him!—As to the happiest *day*, that must be very difficult for any wise man to name: because any event, that could occupy so distinguished a place in a man's retrospect of his life, or be entitled to have shed a special felicity on any one day, ought to be of such an enduring character, as that (accidents apart) it should have continued to shed the same felicity, or one not distinguishably less, on many years together. To the happiest *lustrum*, however, or even to the happiest *year*, it may be allowed to any man to point without discountenance from wisdom. This year, in my case, reader, was the one which we have now reached; though it stood, I confess, as a parenthesis between years of a gloomier character. It was a year of brilliant water (to speak after the manner of jewellers), set as it were, and insulated, in the gloom and cloudy melancholy of opium. Strange as it may sound, I had a little before this time descended suddenly, and without any considerable effort, from 320 grains of opium (i.e. eight * thousand drops of laudanum) per day, to forty grains, or one eighth part. Instantaneously, and as if by magic, the cloud of profoundest melancholy which rested upon my brain, like some black vapours that I have seen roll away from the summits of mountains, drew off in one day (νυχθήμερον); passed off with its murky banners as simultaneously as a ship that has been stranded, and is floated off by a spring tide—

That moveth altogether, if it move at all.

Now, then, I was again happy: I now took only 1000 drops of laudanum per day: and what was that? A latter spring had come to close up the season of youth: my brain performed its functions as healthily as ever before: I read Kant again; and again I understood him, or fancied that I did. Again my feelings of pleasure expanded themselves to all around me: and if any man from Oxford or Cambridge, or from neither, had been announced to me in my unpretending cottage, I should have welcomed him with as sumptuous a reception as so poor a man could offer. Whatever else was wanting to a wise man's happiness,—of laudanum I would have given him as much as he wished, and in a golden cup. And, by the way, now that I speak of giving laudanum away, I remember, about this time, a little incident, which I mention, because, trifling as it was, the reader will soon meet it again in my dreams, which it influenced more fearfully than could be imagined.

* I here reckon twenty-five drops of laudanum as equivalent to one grain of opium, which, I believe, is the common estimate. However, as both may be considered variable quantities (the crude opium varying much in strength, and the tincture still more), I suppose that no infinitesimal accuracy can be had in such a calculation. Tea-spoons vary as much in size as opium in strength. Small ones hold about 100 drops: so that 8000 drops are about eighty times a tea-spoonful. The reader sees how much I kept within Dr. Buchan's indulgent allowance.

One day a Malay knocked at my door. What business a Malay could have to transact amongst English mountains, I cannot conjecture: but possibly he was on his road to a sea-port about forty miles distant.

The servant who opened the door to him was a young girl born and bred amongst the mountains, who had never seen an Asiatic dress of any sort: his turban, therefore, confounded her not a little: and, as it turned out, that his attainments in English were exactly of the same extent as hers in the Malay, there seemed to be an impassable gulph fixed between all communication of ideas, if either party had happened to possess any. In this dilemma, the girl, recollecting the reputed learning of her master (and, doubtless, giving me credit for a knowledge of all the languages of the earth, besides, perhaps, a few of the lunar ones), came and gave me to understand that there was a sort of demon below, whom she clearly imagined that my art could exorcise from the house. I did not immediately go down: but, when I did, the group which presented itself, arranged as it was by accident, though not very elaborate, took hold of my fancy and my eye in a way that none of the statuesque attitudes exhibited in the ballets at the Opera House, though so ostentatiously complex, had ever done. In a cottage kitchen, but panelled on the wall with dark wood that from age and rubbing resembled oak, and looking more like a rustic hall of entrance than a kitchen, stood the Malay—his turban and loose trowsers of dingy white relieved upon the dark panelling: he had placed himself nearer to the girl than she seemed to relish; though her native spirit of mountain intrepidity contended with the feeling of simple awe which her countenance expressed as she gazed upon the tiger-cat before her. And a more striking picture there could not be imagined, than the beautiful English face of the girl, and its exquisite fairness, together with her erect and independent attitude, contrasted with the sallow and bilious skin of the Malay, enamelled or veneered with mahogany, by marine air, his small, fierce, restless eyes, thin lips, slavish gestures and adorations. Half-hidden by the ferocious looking Malay, was a little child from a neighbouring cottage who had crept in after him, and was now in the act of reverting its head, and gazing upwards at the turban and the fiery eyes beneath it, whilst with one hand he caught at the dress of the young woman for protection. My knowledge of the Oriental tongues is not remarkably extensive, being indeed confined to two words—the Arabic word for barley, and the Turkish for opium (madjoon), which I have learned from Anastasius. And, as I had neither a Malay dictionary, nor even Adelung's *Mithridates*, which might have helped me to a few words, I addressed him in some lines from the Iliad; considering that, of such languages as I possessed, Greek, in point of longitude, came geographically nearest to an Oriental one. He worshipped me in a most devout manner, and replied in what I suppose was Malay. In this way I saved my reputation with my neighbours; for the Malay had no means of betraying the secret. He lay down upon the floor for about an hour, and then pursued his journey. On his departure, I presented him with a piece of opium. To him, as an Orientalist, I concluded that opium must be familiar: and the expression of his face convinced me that it was. Nevertheless, I was struck with some little consternation when I saw him suddenly raise his hand to his mouth, and (in the school-boy phrase) bolt the whole, divided into three pieces, at one mouthful. The quantity was enough to kill three dragoons and their horses: and I felt some alarm for the poor creature: but what could be done? I had given him the opium in compassion for his solitary life, on recollecting that if he had travelled on foot from London, it must be nearly three weeks since he could have exchanged a thought with any human being. I could not think of violating the laws of hospitality, by having him seized and drenched with an emetic, and thus frightening him into a notion that we were going to sacrifice him to some English idol. No: there was clearly no help for it:—he took his leave: and for some days I felt anxious: but as I never heard of any Malay being found dead, I became convinced that he was used* to opium: and that I must have done him the service I designed, by giving him one night of respite from the pains of wandering.

This incident I have digressed to mention, because this Malay (partly from the picturesque exhibition he assisted to frame, partly from the anxiety I connected with his image for some days) fastened afterwards upon my dreams, and brought other Malays with him worse than himself, that ran "a-muck"† at me, and led me into a world of troubles.—But to quit this episode, and to return to my intercalary year of happiness. I have said already, that on a subject so important to us all as happiness, we should listen with pleasure to any man's experience or experiments, even though he were but a plough-boy, who cannot be supposed to have ploughed very deep into such an intractable soil as that of human pains and pleasures, or to have conducted his researches upon any very enlightened principles. But I, who have taken happiness, both in a solid and a liquid shape, both boiled and unboiled, both East India and Turkey—who have conducted my experiments upon this interesting subject with a sort of galvanic battery—and

* This, however, is not a necessary conclusion: the varieties of effect produced by opium on different constitutions, are infinite. A London Magistrate (Harriott's *Struggles through Life*, vol. iii, p. 391, Third Edition), has recorded that, on the first occasion of his trying laudanum for the gout, he took *forty* drops, the next night sixty, and on the fifth night *eighty*, without any effect whatever: and this at an advanced age. I have an anecdote from a country surgeon, however, which sinks Mr. Harriott's case into a trifle: and in my projected medical treatise on opium which I will publish, provided the College of Surgeons will pay me for enlightening their benighted understandings upon this subject, I will relate it: but it is far too good a story to be published gratis.

† See the common accounts in any Eastern traveller or voyager of the frantic excesses committed by Malays who have taken opium, or are reduced to desperation by ill luck at gambling.

have, for the general benefit of the world, inoculated myself, as it were, with the poison of 8000 drops of laudanum per day (just, for the same reason, as a French surgeon inoculated himself lately with cancer—an English one, twenty years ago, with plague—and a third, I know not of what nation, with hydrophobia),—*I* (it will be admitted) must surely know what happiness is, if any body does. And, therefore, I will here lay down an analysis of happiness; and as the most interesting mode of communicating it, I will give it, not didactically, but wrapt up and involved in a picture of one evening, as I spent every evening during the intercalary year when laudanum, though taken daily, was to me no more than the elixir of pleasure. This done, I shall quit the subject of happiness altogether, and pass to a very different one—the *pains of opium*.

Let there be a cottage, standing in a valley, 18 miles from any town—no spacious valley, but about two miles long, by three quarters of a mile in average width; the benefit of which provision is, that all the families resident within its circuit will compose, as it were, one larger household personally familiar to your eye, and more or less interesting to your affections. Let the mountains be real mountains, between 3 and 4000 feet high; and the cottage, a real cottage; not (as a witty author has it) "a cottage with a double coach-house:" let it be, in fact (for I must abide by the actual scene), a white cottage, embowered with flowering shrubs, so chosen as to unfold a succession of flowers upon the walls, and clustering round the windows through all the months of spring, summer, and autumn—beginning, in fact, with May roses, and ending with jasmine. Let it, however, *not* be spring, nor summer, nor autumn—but winter, in his sternest shape. This is a most important point in the science of happiness. And I am surprised to see people overlook it, and think it matter of congratulation that winter is going; or, if coming, is not likely to be a severe one. On the contrary, I put up a petition annually, for as much snow, hail, frost, or storm, of one kind or other, as the skies can possibly afford us. Surely every body is aware of the divine pleasures which attend a winter fire-side: candles at four o'clock, warm hearth-rugs, tea, a fair tea-maker, shutters closed, curtains flowing in ample draperies on the floor, whilst the wind and rain are raging audibly without,

> And at the doors and windows seem to call,
> As heav'n and earth they would together mell;
> Yet the least entrance find they none at all;
> Whence sweeter grows our rest secure in massy hall.
> —*Castle of Indolence.*

All these are items in the description of a winter evening, which must surely be familiar to every body born in a high latitude. And it is evident, that most of

52

these delicacies, like ice-cream, require a very low temperature of the atmosphere to produce them: they are fruits which cannot be ripened without weather stormy or inclement, in some way or other. I am not *"particular,"* as people say, whether it be snow, or black frost, or wind so strong, that (as Mr. [Clarkson] says) "you may lean your back against it like a post." I can put up even with rain, provided it rains cats and dogs: but something of the sort I must have: and, if I have it not, I think myself in a manner ill-used: for why am I called on to pay so heavily for winter, in coals, and candles, and various privations that will occur even to gentlemen, if I am not to have the article good of its kind? No: a Canadian winter for my money: or a Russian one, where every man is but a co-proprietor with the north wind in the fee-simple of his own ears. Indeed, so great an epicure am I in this matter, that I cannot relish a winter night fully if it be much past St. Thomas's day, and have degenerated into disgusting tendencies to vernal appearances: no: it must be divided by a thick wall of dark nights from all return of light and sunshine.—From the latter weeks of October to Christmas-eve, therefore, is the period during which happiness is in season, which, in my judgment, enters the room with the tea-tray: for tea, though ridiculed by those who are naturally of coarse nerves, or are become so from wine-drinking, and are not susceptible of influence from so refined a stimulant, will always be the favourite beverage of the intellectual: and, for my part, I would have joined Dr. Johnson in a *bellum internecinum* against Jonas Hanway, or any other impious person, who should presume to disparage it.—But here, to save myself the trouble of too much verbal description, I will introduce a painter; and give him directions for the rest of the picture. Painters do not like white cottages, unless a good deal weather-stained: but as the reader now understands that it is a winter night, his services will not be required, except for the inside of the house.

Paint me, then, a room seventeen feet by twelve, and not more than seven and a half feet high. This, reader, is somewhat ambitiously styled, in my family, the drawing-room: but, being contrived "a double debt to pay," it is also, and more justly, termed the library; for it happens that books are the only article of property in which I am richer than my neighbours. Of these, I have about five thousand, collected gradually since my eighteenth year. Therefore, painter, put as many as you can into this room. Make it populous with books: and, furthermore, paint me a good fire; and furniture, plain and modest, befitting the unpretending cottage of a scholar. And, near the fire, paint me a tea-table; and (as it is clear that no creature can come to see one such a stormy night,) place only two cups and saucers on the tea-tray: and, if you know how to paint such a thing symbolically, or otherwise, paint me an eternal tea-pot—eternal *à parte ante,* and *à parte post;* for I usually drink tea from eight o'clock at night to four o'clock

53

in the morning. And, as it is very unpleasant to make tea, or to pour it out for oneself, paint me a lovely young woman, sitting at the table. Paint her arms like Aurora's, and her smiles like Hebe's:—But no, dear M[argaret], not even in jest let me insinuate that thy power to illuminate my cottage rests upon a tenure so perishable as mere personal beauty; or that the witchcraft of angelic smiles lies within the empire of any earthly pencil. Pass, then, my good painter, to something more within its power: and the next article brought forward should naturally be myself—a picture of the Opium-eater, with his "little golden receptacle of the pernicious drug," lying beside him on the table. As to the opium, I have no objection to see a picture of *that*, though I would rather see the original: you may paint it, if you choose; but I apprize you, that no "little" receptacle would, even in 1816, answer *my* purpose, who was at a distance from the "stately Pantheon," and all druggists (mortal or otherwise). No: you may as well paint the real receptacle, which was not of gold, but of glass, and as much like a wine-decanter as possible. Into this you may put a quart of ruby-coloured laudanum: that, and a book of German metaphysics placed by its side, will sufficiently attest my being in the neighbourhood; but, as to myself,—there I demur. I admit that, naturally, I ought to occupy the foreground of the picture; that being the hero of the piece, or (if you choose) the criminal at the bar, my body should be had into court. This seems reasonable: but why should I confess, on this point, to a painter? or why confess at all? If the public (into whose private ear I am confidentially whispering my confessions, and not into any painter's) should chance to have framed some agreeable picture for itself, of the Opium-eater's exterior,—should have ascribed to him, romantically, an elegant person, or a handsome face, why should I barbarously tear from it so pleasing a delusion—pleasing both to the public and to me? No: paint me, if at all, according to your own fancy: and, as a painter's fancy should teem with beautiful creations, I cannot fail, in that way, to be a gainer. And now, reader, we have run through all the ten categories of my condition, as it stood about 1816—17: up to the middle of which latter year I judge myself to have been a happy man: and the elements of that happiness I have endeavoured to place before you, in the above sketch of the interior of a scholar's library, in a cottage among the mountains, on a stormy winter evening.

But now farewell—a long farewell to happiness—winter or summer! farewell to smiles and laughter! farewell to peace of mind! farewell to hope and to tranquil dreams, and to the blessed consolations of sleep! for more than three years and a half I am summoned away from these: I am now arrived at an Iliad of woes: for I have now to record

THE PAINS OF OPIUM

——as when some great painter dips
His pencil in the gloom of earthquake and eclipse.
SHELLEY'S *Revolt of Islam.*

READER, who have thus far accompanied me, I must request your attention to a brief explanatory note on three points:

1. For several reasons, I have not been able to compose the notes for this part of my narrative into any regular and connected shape. I give the notes disjointed as I find them, or have now drawn them up from memory. Some of them point to their own date; some I have dated; and some are undated. Whenever it could answer my purpose to transplant them from the natural or chronological order, I have not scrupled to do so. Sometimes I speak in the present, sometimes in the past tense. Few of the notes, perhaps, were written exactly at the period of time to which they relate; but this can little affect their accuracy; as the impressions were such that they can never fade from my mind. Much has been omitted. I could not, without effort, constrain myself to the task of either recalling, or constructing into a regular narrative, the whole burthen of horrors which lies upon my brain. This feeling partly I plead in excuse, and partly that I am now in London, and am a helpless sort of person, who cannot even arrange his own papers without assistance; and I am separated from the hands which are wont to perform for me the offices of an amanuensis.

2. You will think, perhaps, that I am too confidential and communicative of my own private history. It may be so. But my way of writing is rather to think aloud, and follow my own humours, than much to consider who is listening to me; and, if I stop to consider what is proper to be said to this or that person, I shall soon come to doubt whether any part at all is proper. The fact is, I place myself at a distance of fifteen or twenty years ahead of this time, and suppose myself writing to those who will be interested about me hereafter; and wishing to have some record of a time, the entire history of which no one can know but myself, I do it as fully as I am able with the efforts I am now capable of making, because I know not whether I can ever find time to do it again.

3. It will occur to you often to ask, why did I not release myself from the horrors of opium, by leaving it off, or diminishing it? To this I must answer briefly: it might be supposed that I yielded to the fascinations of opium too easily; it cannot be supposed that any man can be charmed by its terrors. The reader may be sure, therefore, that I made attempts innumerable to reduce the quantity. I

add, that those who witnessed the agonies of those attempts, and not myself, were the first to beg me to desist. But could not I have reduced it a drop a day, or by adding water, have bisected or trisected a drop? A thousand drops bisected would thus have taken nearly six years to reduce; and that way would certainly not have answered. But this is a common mistake of those who know nothing of opium experimentally; I appeal to those who do, whether it is not always found that down to a certain point it can be reduced with ease and even pleasure, but that, after that point, further reduction causes intense suffering. Yes, say many thoughtless persons, who know not what they are talking of, you will suffer a little low spirits and dejection for a few days. I answer, no; there is nothing like low spirits; on the contrary, the mere animal spirits are uncommonly raised: the pulse is improved: the health is better. It is not there that the suffering lies. It has no resemblance to the sufferings caused by renouncing wine. It is a state of unutterable irritation of stomach (which surely is not much like dejection), accompanied by intense perspirations, and feelings such as I shall not attempt to describe without more space at my command.

I shall now enter *"in medias res,"* and shall anticipate, from a time when my opium pains might be said to be at their *acmé*, an account of their palsying effects on the intellectual faculties.

MY STUDIES have now been long interrupted. I cannot read to myself with any pleasure, hardly with a moment's endurance. Yet I read aloud sometimes for the pleasure of others; because, reading is an accomplishment of mine; and, in the slang use of the word *accomplishment* as a superficial and ornamental attainment, almost the only one I possess: and formerly, if I had any vanity at all connected with any endowment or attainment of mine, it was with this; for I had observed that no accomplishment was so rare. Players are the worst readers of all: [John Kemble] reads vilely: and Mrs. [Siddons], who is so celebrated, can read nothing well but dramatic compositions: Milton she cannot read sufferably. People in general either read poetry without any passion at all, or else overstep the modesty of nature, and read not like scholars. Of late, if I have felt moved by anything in books, it has been by the grand lamentations of Samson Agonistes, or the great harmonies of the Satanic speeches in Paradise Regained, when read aloud by myself. A young lady sometimes comes and drinks tea with us: at her request and M[argaret]'s I now and then·read W[ordsworth]'s poems to them. (W[ordsworth] by the bye, is the only poet I ever met who could read his own verses: often indeed he reads admirably.)

56

For nearly two years I believe that I read no book but one: and I owe it to the author, in discharge of a great debt of gratitude, to mention what that was. The sublimer and more passionate poets I still read, as I have said, by snatches, and occasionally. But my proper vocation, as I well knew, was the exercise of the analytic understanding. Now, for the most part, analytic studies are continuous, and not to be pursued by fits and starts, or fragmentary efforts. Mathematics, for instance, intellectual philosophy, &c. were all become insupportable to me; I shrunk from them with a sense of powerless and infantine feebleness that gave me an anguish the greater from remembering the time when I grappled with them to my own hourly delight; and for this further reason, because I had devoted the labour of my whole life, and had dedicated my intellect, blossoms and fruits, to the slow and elaborate toil of constructing one single work, to which I had presumed to give the title of an unfinished work of Spinosa's; viz. *De emendatione humani intellectûs*. This was now lying locked up, as by frost, like any Spanish bridge or aqueduct, begun upon too great a scale for the resources of the architect; and, instead of surviving me as a monument of wishes at least, and aspirations, and a life of labour dedicated to the exaltation of human nature in that way in which God had best fitted me to promote so great an object, it was likely to stand a memorial to my children of hopes defeated, of baffled efforts, of materials uselessly accumulated, of foundations laid that were never to support a superstructure,—of the grief and the ruin of the architect. In this state of imbecility, I had, for amusement, turned my attention to political economy; my understanding, which formerly had been as active and restless as a hyena, could not, I suppose (so long as I lived at all) sink into utter lethargy; and political economy offers this advantage to a person in my state, that though it is eminently an organic science (no part, that is to say, but what acts on the whole, as the whole again re-acts on each part), yet the several parts may be detached and contemplated singly. Great as was the prostration of my powers at this time, yet I could not forget my knowledge; and my understanding had been for too many years intimate with severe thinkers, with logic, and the great masters of knowledge, not to be aware of the utter feebleness of the main herd of modern economists. I had been led in 1811 to look into loads of books and pamphlets on many branches of economy; and, at my desire, M[argaret] sometimes read to me chapters from more recent works, or parts of parliamentary debates. I saw that these were generally the very dregs and rinsings of the human intellect; and that any man of sound head, and practised in wielding logic with a scholastic adroitness, might take up the whole academy of modern economists, and throttle them between heaven and earth with his finger and thumb, or bray their fungus heads to powder with a lady's fan. At length, in 1819, a friend in Edinburgh sent me down Mr. Ricardo's book: and recurring to my own prophetic anticipation of the advent of some legislator for this science, I said, before I had finished the first chapter, "Thou art the man!" Wonder and curiosity were emotions that had long been dead in me. Yet I wondered once more: I wondered at myself that I could once again be stimulated to the effort of reading: and much more I wondered at the book. Had this profound work been really written in England during the nineteenth century? Was it possible? I supposed thinking* had been extinct in England. Could it be that an Englishman, and he not in academic bowers, but oppressed by mercantile and senatorial cares, had accomplished what all the universities of Europe, and a century of thought, had failed even to advance by one hair's breadth? All other writers had been crushed and overlaid by the enormous weight of facts and documents; Mr. Ricardo had deduced, *à priori*, from the understanding itself, laws which first gave a ray of light into the unwieldy chaos of materials, and had constructed what had been but a collection of tentative discussions into a science of regular proportions, now first standing on an eternal basis.

Thus did one single work of a profound understanding avail to give me a pleasure and an activity which I had not known for years:—it roused me even to write, or, at least, to dictate, what M[argaret] wrote for me. It seemed to me, that some important truths had escaped even "the inevitable eye" of Mr. Ricardo: and, as these were, for the most part, of such a nature that I could express or illustrate them more briefly and elegantly by algebraic symbols than in the usual clumsy and loitering diction of economists, the whole would not have filled a pocket-book; and being so brief, with M[argaret] for my amanuensis, even at this time, incapable as I was of all general exertion, I drew up my *Prolegomena to all future Systems of Political Economy.* I hope it will not be found redolent of opium; though, indeed, to most people, the subject itself is a sufficient opiate.

This exertion, however, was but a temporary flash; as the sequel showed—for I designed to publish my work: arrangements were made at a provincial press, about eighteen miles distant, for printing it. An additional compositor was retained, for some days, on this account. The work was even twice advertised: and I was, in a manner, pledged to the fulfilment of my intention. But I had a preface to write; and a dedication, which I wished to make a splendid one, to Mr. Ri-

---

* The reader must remember what I here mean by *thinking*: because, else this would be a very presumptuous expression. England, of late, has been rich to excess in fine thinkers, in the departments of creative and combining thought; but there is a sad dearth of masculine thinkers in any analytic path. A Scotchman of eminent name has lately told us, that he is obliged to quit even mathematics, for want of encouragement.

cardo. I found myself quite unable to accomplish all this. The arrangements were countermanded: the compositor dismissed: and my "Prolegomena" rested peacefully by the side of its elder and more dignified brother.

I have thus described and illustrated my intellectual torpor, in terms that apply, more or less, to every part of the four years during which I was under the Circean spells of opium. But for misery and suffering, I might, indeed, be said to have existed in a dormant state. I seldom could prevail on myself to write a letter; an answer of a few words, to any that I received, was the utmost that I could accomplish; and often *that* not until the letter had lain weeks, or even months, on my writing table. Without the aid of M [argaret] all records of bills paid, or *to be* paid, must have perished: and my whole domestic economy, whatever became of Political Economy, must have gone into irretrievable confusion.—I shall not afterwards allude to this part of the case: it is one, however, which the opium-eater will find, in the end, as oppressive and tormenting as any other, from the sense of incapacity and feebleness, from the direct embarrassments incident to the neglect or procrastination of each day's appropriate duties, and from the remorse which must often exasperate the stings of these evils to a reflective and conscientious mind. The opium-eater loses none of his moral sensibilities, or aspirations: he wishes and longs, as earnestly as ever, to realize what he believes possible, and feels to be exacted by duty; but his intellectual apprehension of what is possible infinitely outruns his power, not of execution only, but even of power to attempt. He lies under the weight of incubus and night-mare: he lies in sight of all that he would fain perform, just as a man forcibly confined to his bed by the mortal languor of a relaxing disease, who is compelled to witness injury or outrage offered to some object of his tenderest love:—he curses the spells which chain him down from motion:—he would lay down his life if he might but get up and walk; but he is powerless as an infant, and cannot even attempt to rise.

I now pass to what is the main subject of these latter confessions, to the history and journal of what took place in my dreams; for these were the immediate and proximate cause of my acutest suffering.

The first notice I had of any important change going on in this part of my physical economy, was from the re-awakening of a state of eye generally incident to childhood, or exalted states of irritability. I know not whether my reader is aware that many children, perhaps most, have a power of painting, as it were, upon the darkness, all sorts of phantoms; in some, that power is simply a mechanic affection of the eye; others have a voluntary, or a semi-voluntary power to dismiss or to summon them; or, as a child once said to me when I questioned him on this matter, "I can tell them to go, and they go; but sometimes they

59

come, when I don't tell them to come." Whereupon I told him that he had almost as unlimited a command over apparitions, as a Roman centurion over his soldiers.—In the middle of 1817, I think it was, that this faculty became positively distressing to me: at night, when I lay awake in bed, vast processions passed along in mournful pomp; friezes of never-ending stories, that to my feelings were as sad and solemn as if they were stories drawn from times before Œdipus or Priam—before Tyre—before Memphis. And, at the same time, a corresponding change took place in my dreams; a theatre seemed suddenly opened and lighted up within my brain, which presented nightly spectacles of more than earthly splendour. And the four following facts may be mentioned, as noticeable at this time:

1. That, as the creative state of the eye increased, a sympathy seemed to arise between the waking and the dreaming states of the brain in one point—that whatsoever I happened to call up and to trace by a voluntary act upon the darkness was very apt to transfer itself to my dreams; so that I feared to exercise this faculty; for, as Midas turned all things to gold, that yet baffled his hopes and defrauded his human desires, so whatsoever things capable of being visually represented I did but think of in the darkness, immediately shaped themselves into phantoms of the eye; and, by a process apparently no less inevitable, when thus once traced in faint and visionary colours, like writings in sympathetic ink, they were drawn out by the fierce chemistry of my dreams, into insufferable splendour that fretted my heart.

2. For this, and all other changes in my dreams, were accompanied by deep-seated anxiety and gloomy melancholy, such as are wholly incommunicable by words. I seemed every night to descend, not metaphorically, but literally to descend, into chasms and sunless abysses, depths below depths, from which it seemed hopeless that I could ever re-ascend. Nor did I, by waking, feel that I *had* re-ascended. This I do not dwell upon; because the state of gloom which attended these gorgeous spectacles, amounting at last to utter darkness, as of some suicidal despondency, cannot be approached by words.

3. The sense of space, and in the end, the sense of time, were both powerfully affected. Buildings, landscapes, &c. were exhibited in proportions so vast as the bodily eye is not fitted to receive. Space swelled, and was amplified to an extent of unutterable infinity. This, however, did not disturb me so much as the vast expansion of time; I sometimes seemed to have lived for 70 or 100 years in one night; nay, sometimes had feelings representative of a millennium passed in that time, or, however, of a duration far beyond the limits of any human experience.

4. The minutest incidents of childhood, or forgotten scenes of later years, were often revived: I could not be said to recollect them; for if I had been told of them when waking, I should not have been able to acknowledge them as parts

of my past experience. But placed as they were before me, in dreams like intuitions, and clothed in all their evanescent circumstances and accompanying feelings, I *recognised* them instantaneously. I was once told by a near relative of mine, that having in her childhood fallen into a river, and being on the very verge of death but for the critical assistance which reached her, she saw in a moment her whole life, in its minutest incidents, arrayed before her simultaneously as in a mirror; and she had a faculty developed as suddenly for comprehending the whole and every part. This, from some opium experiences of mine, I can believe; I have, indeed, seen the same thing asserted twice in modern books, and accompanied by a remark which I am convinced is true; viz. that the dread book of account, which the Scriptures speak of, is, in fact, the mind itself of each individual. Of this at least, I feel assured, that there is no such thing as *forgetting* possible to the mind; a thousand accidents may, and will interpose a veil between our present consciousness and the secret inscriptions on the mind; accidents of the same sort will also rend away this veil; but alike, whether veiled or unveiled, the inscription remains for ever; just as the stars seem to withdraw before the common light of day, whereas, in fact, we all know that it is the light which is drawn over them as a veil—and that they are waiting to be revealed when the obscuring daylight shall have withdrawn.

Having noticed these four facts as memorably distinguishing my dreams from those of health, I shall now cite a case illustrative of the first fact; and shall then cite any others that I remember, either in their chronological order, or any other that may give them more effect as pictures to the reader.

I had been in youth, and even since, for occasional amusement, a great reader of Livy, whom, I confess, that I prefer, both for style and matter, to any other of the Roman historians: and I had often felt as most solemn and appalling sounds, and most emphatically representative of the majesty of the Roman people, the two words so often occurring in Livy—*Consul Romanus;* especially when the consul is introduced in his military character. I mean to say, that the words king—sultan—regent, &c. or any other titles of those who embody in their own persons the collective majesty of a great people, had less power over my reverential feelings. I had also, though no great reader of history, made myself minutely and critically familiar with one period of English history, viz. the period of the Parliamentary War, having been attracted by the moral grandeur of some who figured in that day, and by the many interesting memoirs which survive those unquiet times. Both these parts of my lighter reading, having furnished me often with matter of reflection, now furnished me with matter for my dreams. Often I used to see, after painting upon the blank darkness a sort of rehearsal whilst waking, a crowd of ladies, and perhaps a festival, and dances. And I heard it said, or I said to myself, "these are English ladies from the unhappy times of Charles I. These are the wives and the daughters of those who met in peace, and sate at the same tables, and were allied by marriage or by blood; and yet, after a certain day in August, 1642, never smiled upon each other again, nor met but in the field of battle; and at Marston Moor, at Newbury, or at Naseby, cut asunder all ties of love by the cruel sabre, and washed away in blood the memory of ancient friendship."—The ladies danced, and looked as lovely as the court of George IV. Yet I knew, even in my dream, that they had been in the grave for nearly two centuries.—This pageant would suddenly dissolve: and, at a clapping of hands, would be heard the heart-quaking sound of *Consul Romanus:* and immediately came "sweeping by," in gorgeous paludaments, Paulus or Marius, girt round by a company of centurions, with the crimson tunic hoisted on a spear, and followed by the *alalagmos* of the Roman legions.

Many years ago, when I was looking over Piranesi's Antiquities of Rome, Mr. Coleridge, who was standing by, described to me a set of plates by that artist, called his *Dreams,* and which record the scenery of his own visions during the delirium of a fever. Some of them (I describe only from memory of Mr. Coleridge's account) represented vast Gothic halls: on the floor of which stood all sorts of engines and machinery, wheels, cables, pulleys, levers, catapults, &c. &c. expressive of enormous power put forth, and resistance overcome. Creeping along the sides of the walls, you perceived a staircase; and upon it, groping his way upwards, was Piranesi himself: follow the stairs a little further, and you perceive it come to a sudden abrupt termination, without any balustrade, and allowing no step onwards to him who had reached the extremity, except into the depths below. Whatever is to become of poor Piranesi, you suppose, at least, that his labours must in some way terminate here. But raise your eyes, and behold a second flight of stairs still higher: on which again Piranesi is perceived, but this time standing on the very brink of the abyss. Again elevate your eye, and a still more aerial flight of stairs is beheld: and again is poor Piranesi busy on his aspiring labours: and so on, until the unfinished stairs and Piranesi both are lost in the upper gloom of the hall.—With the same power of endless growth and self-reproduction did my architecture proceed in dreams. In the early stage of my malady, the splendours of my dreams were indeed chiefly architectural: and I beheld such pomp of cities and palaces as was never yet beheld by the waking eye, unless in the clouds. From a great modern poet I cite part of a passage which describes, as an appearance actually beheld in the clouds, what in many of its circumstances I saw frequently in sleep:

62

The appearance, instantaneously disclosed,
Was of a mighty city—boldly say
A wilderness of building, sinking far
And self-withdrawn into a wondrous depth,
Far sinking into splendor—without end!
Fabric it seem'd of diamond, and of gold,
With alabaster domes, and silver spires,
And blazing terrace upon terrace, high
Uplifted; here, serene pavilions bright
In avenues disposed; there towers begirt
With battlements that on their restless fronts
Bore stars—illumination of all gems!
By earthly nature had the effect been wrought
Upon the dark materials of the storm
Now pacified; on them, and on the coves,
And mountain-steeps and summits, whereunto
The vapours had receded,—taking there
Their station under a cerulean sky. &c. &c.

The sublime circumstance—"battlements that on their *restless* fronts bore stars,"—might have been copied from my architectural dreams, for it often occurred.—We hear it reported of Dryden, and of Fuseli in modern times, that they thought proper to eat raw meat for the sake of obtaining splendid dreams: how much better for such a purpose to have eaten opium, which yet I do not remember that any poet is recorded to have done, except the dramatist Shadwell: and in ancient days, Homer is, I think, rightly reputed to have known the virtues of opium.

To my architecture succeeded dreams of lakes—and silvery expanses of water: —these haunted me so much, that I feared (though possibly it will appear ludicrous to a medical man) that some dropsical state or tendency of the brain might thus be making itself (to use a metaphysical word) *objective;* and the sentient organ *project* itself as its own object.—For two months I suffered greatly in my head,—a part of my bodily structure which had hitherto been so clear from all touch or taint of weakness (physically, I mean), that I used to say of it, as the last Lord Orford said of his stomach, that it seemed likely to survive the rest of my person.—Till now I had never felt a head-ach even, or any the slightest pain, except rheumatic pains caused by my own folly. However, I got over this attack, though it must have been verging on something very dangerous.

The waters now changed their character,—from translucent lakes, shining like mirrors, they now became seas and oceans. And now came a tremendous change, which, unfolding itself slowly like a scroll, through many months, promised an abiding torment; and, in fact, it never left me until the winding up of my case. Hitherto the human face had mixed often in my dreams, but not despotically, nor with any special power of tormenting. But now that which I have called the tyranny of the human face began to unfold itself. Perhaps some part of my London life might be answerable for this. Be that as it may, now it was that upon the rocking waters of the ocean the human face began to appear: the sea appeared paved with innumerable faces, upturned to the heavens: faces, imploring, wrathful, despairing, surged upwards by thousands, by myriads, by generations, by centuries:—my agitation was infinite,—my mind tossed—and surged with the ocean.

May, 1818.

THE MALAY has been a fearful enemy for months. I have been every night, through his means, transported into Asiatic scenes. I know not whether others share in my feelings on this point; but I have often thought that if I were compelled to forego England, and to live in China, and among Chinese manners and modes of life and scenery, I should go mad. The causes of my horror lie deep; and some of them must be common to others. Southern Asia, in general, is the seat of awful images and associations. As the cradle of the human race, it would alone have a dim and reverential feeling connected with it. But there are other reasons. No man can pretend that the wild, barbarous, and capricious superstitions of Africa, or of savage tribes elsewhere, affect him in the way that he is affected by the ancient, monumental, cruel, and elaborate religions of Indostan, &c. The mere antiquity of Asiatic things, of their institutions, histories, modes of faith, &c. is so impressive, that to me the vast age of the race and name overpowers the sense of youth in the individual. A young Chinese seems to me an antediluvian man renewed. Even Englishmen, though not bred in any knowledge of such institutions, cannot but shudder at the mystic sublimity of *castes* that have flowed apart, and refused to mix, through such immemorial tracts of time; nor can any man fail to be awed by the names of the Ganges, or the Euphrates. It contributes much to these feelings, that southern Asia is, and has been for thousands of years, the part of the earth most swarming with human life; the great *officina gentium.* Man is a weed in those regions. The vast empires also, into which the enormous population of Asia has always been cast, give a further sub-

64

limity to the feelings associated with all oriental names or images. In China, over and above what it has in common with the rest of southern Asia, I am terrified by the modes of life, by the manners, and the barrier of utter abhorrence, and want of sympathy, placed between us by feelings deeper than I can analyze. I could sooner live with lunatics, or brute animals. All this, and much more than I can say, or have time to say, the reader must enter into before he can comprehend the unimaginable horror which these dreams of oriental imagery, and mythological tortures, impressed upon me. Under the connecting feeling of tropical heat and vertical sun-lights, I brought together all creatures, birds, beasts, reptiles, all trees and plants, usages and appearances, that are found in all tropical regions, and assembled them together in China or Indostan. From kindred feelings, I soon brought Egypt and all her gods under the same law. I was stared at, hooted at, grinned at, chattered at, by monkeys, by paroquets, by cockatoos. I ran into pagodas: and was fixed, for centuries, at the summit, or in secret rooms; I was the idol; I was the priest; I was worshipped; I was sacrificed. I fled from the wrath of Brama through all the forests of Asia: Vishnu hated me: Seeva laid wait for me. I came suddenly upon Isis and Osiris: I had done a deed, they said, which the ibis and the crocodile trembled at. I was buried, for a thousand years, in stone coffins, with mummies and sphynxes, in narrow chambers at the heart of eternal pyramids. I was kissed, with cancerous kisses, by crocodiles; and laid, confounded with all unutterable slimy things, amongst reeds and Nilotic mud.

I thus give the reader some slight abstraction of my oriental dreams, which always filled me with such amazement at the monstrous scenery, that horror seemed absorbed, for a while, in sheer astonishment. Sooner or later, came a reflux of feeling that swallowed up the astonishment, and left me, not so much in terror, as in hatred and abomination of what I saw Over every form, and threat, and punishment, and dim sightless incarceration, brooded a sense of eternity and infinity that drove me into an oppression as of madness. Into these dreams only, it was, with one or two slight exceptions, that any circumstances of physical horror entered. All before had been moral and spiritual terrors. But here the main agents were ugly birds, or snakes, or crocodiles; especially the last. The cursed crocodile became to me the object of more horror than almost all the rest. I was compelled to live with him; and (as was always the case almost in my dreams) for centuries. I escaped sometimes, and found myself in Chinese houses, with cane tables, &c. All the feet of the tables, sophas, &c. soon became instinct with life: the abominable head of the crocodile, and his leering eyes, looked out at me, multiplied into a thousand repetitions: and I stood loathing and fascinated. And so often did this hideous reptile haunt my dreams, that many times the very same dream was broken up in the very same way: I heard gentle voices speaking to me (I hear every thing when I am sleeping); and instantly I awoke: it was broad noon; and my children were standing, hand in hand, at my bed-side; come to show me their coloured shoes, or new frocks, or to let me see them dressed for going out. I protest that so awful was the transition from the damned crocodile, and the other unutterable monsters and abortions of my dreams, to the sight of innocent *human* natures and of infancy, that, in the mighty and sudden revulsion of mind, I wept, and could not forbear it, as I kissed their faces.

June, 1819.

I HAVE had occasion to remark, at various periods of my life, that the deaths of those whom we love, and indeed the contemplation of death generally, is (*cæteris paribus*) more affecting in summer than in any other season of the year. And the reasons are these three, I think: first, that the visible heavens in summer appear far higher, more distant, and (if such a solecism may be excused) more infinite; the clouds, by which chiefly the eye expounds the distance of the blue pavilion stretched over our heads, are in summer more voluminous, massed, and accumulated in far grander and more towering piles: secondly, the light and the appearances of the declining and the setting sun are much more fitted to be types and characters of the Infinite: and, thirdly, (which is the main reason) the exuberant and riotous prodigality of life naturally forces the mind more powerfully upon the antagonist thought of death, and the wintry sterility of the grave. For it may be observed, generally, that wherever two thoughts stand related to each other by a law of antagonism, and exist, as it were, by mutual repulsion, they are apt to suggest each other. On these accounts it is that I find it impossible to banish the thought of death when I am walking alone in the endless days of summer; and any particular death, if not more affecting, at least haunts my mind more obstinately and besiegingly in that season. Perhaps this cause, and a slight incident which I omit, might have been the immediate occasions of the following dream; to which, however, a predisposition must always have existed in my mind; but having been once roused, it never left me, and split into a thousand fantastic varieties, which often suddenly re-united, and composed again the original dream.

I thought that it was a Sunday morning in May, that it was Easter Sunday, and as yet very early in the morning. I was standing, as it seemed to me, at the door of my own cottage. Right before me lay the very scene which could really be commanded from that situation, but exalted, as was usual, and solemnized by

66

the power of dreams. There were the same mountains, and the same lovely valley at their feet; but the mountains were raised to more than Alpine height, and there was interspace far larger between them of meadows and forest lawns; the hedges were rich with white roses; and no living creature was to be seen, excepting that in the green church-yard there were cattle tranquilly reposing upon the verdant graves, and particularly round about the grave of a child whom I had tenderly loved, just as I had really beheld them, a little before sun-rise in the same summer, when that child died. I gazed upon the well-known scene, and I said aloud (as I thought) to myself, "it yet wants much of sun-rise; and it is Easter Sunday; and that is the day on which they celebrate the first fruits of resurrection. I will walk abroad; old griefs shall be forgotten to-day; for the air is cool and still, and the hills are high, and stretch away to Heaven; and the forest-glades are as quiet as the church-yard; and, with the dew, I can wash the fever from my forehead, and then I shall be unhappy no longer." And I turned, as if to open my garden gate; and immediately I saw upon the left a scene far different; but which yet the power of dreams had reconciled into harmony with the other. The scene was an oriental one; and there also it was Easter Sunday, and very early in the morning. And at a vast distance were visible, as a stain upon the horizon, the domes and cupolas of a great city—an image or faint abstraction, caught perhaps in childhood from some picture of Jerusalem. And not a bow-shot from me, upon a stone, and shaded by Judean palms, there sat a woman; and I looked; and it was—Ann! She fixed her eyes upon me earnestly; and I said to her at length: "So then I have found you at last." I waited: but she answered me not a word. Her face was the same as when I saw it last, and yet again how different! Seventeen years ago, when the lamp-light fell upon her face, as for the last time I kissed her lips (lips, Ann, that to me were not polluted), her eyes were streaming with tears: the tears were now wiped away; she seemed more beautiful than she was at that time, but in all other points the same, and not older. Her looks were tranquil, but with unusual solemnity of expression; and I now gazed upon her with some awe, but suddenly her countenance grew dim, and, turning to the mountains, I perceived vapours rolling between us; in a moment, all had vanished; thick darkness came on; and, in the twinkling of an eye, I was far away from mountains, and by lamp-light in Oxford-street, walking again with Ann—just as we walked seventeen years before, when we were both children.

As a final specimen, I cite one of a different character, from 1820.

The dream commenced with a music which now I often heard in dreams—a music of preparation and of awakening suspense; a music like the opening of the Coronation Anthem, and which, like *that*, gave the feeling of a vast march—of

infinite cavalcades filing off—and the tread of innumerable armies. The morning
was come of a mighty day—a day of crisis and of final hope for human nature,
then suffering some mysterious eclipse, and labouring in some dread extremity.
Somewhere, I knew not where—somehow, I knew not how—by some beings, I
knew not whom—a battle, a strife, an agony, was conducting,—was evolving like
a great drama, or piece of music; with which my sympathy was the more insupportable from my confusion as to its place, its cause, its nature, and its possible
issue. I, as is usual in dreams (where, of necessity, we make ourselves central to
every movement), had the power, and yet had not the power, to decide it. I had
the power, if I could raise myself, to will it; and yet again had not the power, for
the weight of twenty Atlantics was upon me, or the oppression of inexpiable
guilt. "Deeper than ever plummet sounded," I lay inactive. Then, like a chorus,
the passion deepened. Some greater interest was at stake; some mightier cause
than ever yet the sword had pleaded, or trumpet had proclaimed. Then came
sudden alarms: hurryings to and fro: trepidations of innumerable fugitives, I
knew not whether from the good cause or the bad: darkness and lights: tempest
and human faces; and at last, with the sense that all was lost, female forms, and
the features that were worth all the world to me, and but a moment allowed,—
and clasped hands, and heart-breaking partings, and then—everlasting farewells!
and with a sigh, such as the caves of hell sighed when the incestuous mother uttered the abhorred name of death, the sound was reverberated—everlasting farewells! and again, and yet again reverberated—everlasting farewells!

And I awoke in struggles, and cried aloud—"I will sleep no more."

BUT I am now called upon to wind up a narrative which has already extended to an unreasonable length. Within more spacious limits, the materials
which I have used might have been better unfolded; and much which I have
not used might have been added with effect. Perhaps, however, enough has been
given. It now remains that I should say something of the way in which this conflict
of horrors was finally brought to a crisis. The reader is already aware (from a passage near the beginning of the introduction to the first part) that the opium-eater
has, in some way or other, "unwound, almost to its final links, the accursed chain
which bound him." By what means? To have narrated this, according to the original intention, would have far exceeded the space which can now be allowed. It is
fortunate, as such a cogent reason exists for abridging it, that I should, on a maturer view of the case, have been exceedingly unwilling to injure, by any such un-
affecting details, the impression of the history itself, as an appeal to the prudence
and the conscience of the yet unconfirmed opium-eater—or even (though a very

68

inferior consideration) to injure its effect as a composition. The interest of the
judicious reader will not attach itself chiefly to the subject of the fascinating
spells, but to the fascinating power. Not the opium-eater, but the opium, is the
true hero of the tale; and the legitimate centre on which the interest revolves.
The object was to display the marvellous agency of opium, whether for pleasure
or for pain: if that is done, the action of the piece has closed.

However, as some people, in spite of all laws to the contrary, will persist in
asking what became of the opium-eater, and in what state he now is, I answer
for him thus: The reader is aware that opium had long ceased to found its empire on spells of pleasure; it was solely by the tortures connected with the attempt
to abjure it, that it kept its hold. Yet, as other tortures, no less it may be thought,
attended the non-abjuration of such a tyrant, a choice only of evils was left; and
that might as well have been adopted, which, however terrific in itself, held out
a prospect of final restoration to happiness. This appears true; but good logic
gave the author no strength to act upon it. However, a crisis arrived for the author's life, and a crisis for other objects still dearer to him—and which will always be far dearer to him than his life, even now that it is again a happy one.—I
saw that I must die if I continued the opium: I determined, therefore, if that
should be required, to die in throwing it off. How much I was at that time taking
I cannot say; for the opium which I used had been purchased for me by a friend
who afterwards refused to let me pay him; so that I could not ascertain even what
quantity I had used within the year. I apprehend, however, that I took it very
irregularly: and that I varied from about fifty or sixty grains, to 150 a-day. My
first task was to reduce it to forty, to thirty, and, as fast as I could, to twelve
grains.

I triumphed: but think not, reader, that therefore my sufferings were ended;
nor think of me as of one sitting in a *dejected* state. Think of me as one, even
when four months had passed, still agitated, writhing, throbbing, palpitating,
shattered; and much, perhaps, in the situation of him who has been racked, as I
collect the torments of that state from the affecting account of them left by a
most innocent sufferer * (of the times of James I.). Meantime, I derived no benefit
from any medicine, except one prescribed to me by an Edinburgh surgeon of great
eminence, viz. ammoniated tincture of Valerian. Medical account, therefore, of
my emancipation I have not much to give: and even that little, as managed by a
man so ignorant of medicine as myself, would probably tend only to mislead.
At all events, it would be misplaced in this situation. The moral of the narrative

* William Lithgow: his book (Travels, &c.) is   his own suffering son the rack at Malaga is over-
ill and pedantically written: but the account of   poweringly affecting.

is addressed to the opium-eater; and therefore, of necessity, limited in its application. If he is taught to fear and tremble, enough has been effected. But he may say, that the issue of my case is at least a proof that opium, after a seventeen years' use, and an eight years' abuse of its powers, may still be renounced: and that *he* may chance to bring to the task greater energy than I did, or that with a stronger constitution than mine he may obtain the same results with less. This may be true: I would not presume to measure the efforts of other men by my own: I heartily wish him more energy: I wish him the same success. Nevertheless, I had motives external to myself which he may unfortunately want: and these supplied me with conscientious supports which mere personal interests might fail to supply to a mind debilitated by opium.

Jeremy Taylor conjectures that it may be as painful to be born as to die: I think it probable: and, during the whole period of diminishing the opium, I had the torments of a man passing out of one mode of existence into another. The issue was not death, but a sort of physical regeneration: and I may add, that ever since, at intervals, I have had a restoration of more than youthful spirits, though under the pressure of difficulties, which, in a less happy state of mind, I should have called misfortunes.

One memorial of my former condition still remains: my dreams are not yet perfectly calm: the dread swell and agitation of the storm have not wholly subsided: the legions that encamped in them are drawing off, but not all departed: my sleep is still tumultuous, and, like the gates of Paradise to our first parents when looking back from afar, it is still (in the tremendous line of Milton)—

With dreadful faces throng'd and fiery arms.

APPENDIX

THE PROPRIETORS of this little work having determined on reprinting it, some explanation seems called for, to account for the non-appearance of a Third Part promised in the LONDON MAGAZINE of December last; and the more so, because the Proprietors, under whose guarantee that promise was issued, might otherwise be implicated in the blame—little or much—attached to its non-fulfilment. This blame, in mere justice, the author takes wholly upon himself. What may be the exact amount of the guilt which he thus appropriates, is a very dark question to his own judgment, and not much illuminated by any of the masters in casuistry whom he has consulted on the occasion. On the one hand it seems generally agreed that a promise is binding in the *inverse* ratio of the numbers to whom it is made: for which reason it is that we see many persons break promise without scruple that are made to a whole nation, who keep their faith religiously in all private engagements,—breaches of promise towards the stronger party being committed at a man's own peril: on the other hand, the only parties interested in the promises of an author are his readers; and these it is a point of modesty in any author to believe as few as possible; or perhaps only one, in which case any promise imposes a sanctity of moral obligation which it is shocking to think of. Casuistry dismissed however,—the author throws himself on the indulgent consideration of all who may conceive themselves aggrieved by his delay—in the following account of his own condition from the end of last year, when the engagement was made, up nearly to the present time. For any purpose of self-excuse, it might be sufficient to say that intolerable bodily suffering had totally disabled him for almost any exertion of mind, more especially for such as demand and presuppose a pleasurable and genial state of feeling: but, as a case that may by possibility contribute a trifle to the medical history of Opium, in a further stage of its action than can often have been brought under the notice of professional men, he has judged that it might be acceptable to some readers to have it described more at length. *Fiat experimentum in corpore vili* is a just rule where there is any reasonable presumption of benefit to arise on a large scale; what the benefit may be, will admit of a doubt: but there can be none as to the value of the body: for a more worthless body than his own, the author is free to confess, cannot be: it is his pride to believe—that it is the very ideal of a base, crazy, despicable human system—that hardly ever could have been meant to be sea-worthy for two days under the ordinary storms and wear-and-tear of

71

life: and indeed, if that were the creditable way of disposing of human bodies, he must own that he should almost be ashamed to bequeath his wretched structure to any respectable dog.—But now to the case; which, for the sake of avoiding the constant recurrence of a cumbersome periphrasis, the author will take the liberty of giving in the first person.

THOSE who have read the Confessions will have closed them with the impression that I had wholly renounced the use of Opium. This impression I meant to convey: and that for two reasons: first, because the very act of deliberately recording such a state of suffering necessarily presumes in the recorder a power of surveying his own case as a cool spectator, and a degree of spirits for adequately describing it, which it would be inconsistent to suppose in any person speaking from the station of an actual sufferer: secondly, because I, who had descended from so large a quantity as 8,000 drops to so small a one (comparatively speaking) as a quantity ranging between 300 and 160 drops, might well suppose that the victory was in effect achieved. In suffering my readers, therefore, to think of me as of a reformed Opium-eater, I left no impression but what I shared myself; and, as may be seen, even this impression was left to be collected from the general tone of the conclusion, and not from any specific words—which are in no instance at variance with the literal truth.—In no long time after that paper was written, I became sensible that the effort which remained would cost me far more energy than I had anticipated: and the necessity for making it was more apparent every month. In particular I became aware of an increasing callousness or defect of sensibility in the stomach; and this I imagined might imply a schirrous state of that organ either formed or forming. An eminent physician, to whose kindness I was at that time deeply indebted, informed me that such a termination of my case was not impossible, though likely to be forestalled by a different termination, in the event of my continuing the use of opium. Opium therefore I resolved wholly to abjure, as soon as I should find myself at liberty to bend my undivided attention and energy to this purpose. It was not however until the 24th of June last that any tolerable concurrence of facilities for such an attempt arrived. On that day I began my experiment, having previously settled in my own mind that I would not flinch, but would "stand up to the scratch"— under any possible "punishment." I must premise that about 170 or 180 drops had been my ordinary allowance for many months: occasionally I had run up as high as 500; and once nearly to 700: in repeated preludes to my final experiment I had also gone as low as 100 drops; but had found it impossible to stand it beyond the 4th day—which, by the way, I have always found more difficult to get over than any of the preceding three. I went off under easy sail—130 drops a day for three days: on the fourth I plunged at once to 80: the misery which I now suffered "took the conceit" out of me at once: and for about a month I continued off and on about this mark: then I sunk to 60: and the next day to— none at all. This was the first day for nearly ten years that I had existed without opium. I persevered in my abstinence for 90 hours; i.e. upwards of half a week. Then I took—ask me not how much: say, ye severest, what would ye have done? Then I abstained again: then took about 25 drops: then abstained: and so on.

Meantime the symptoms which attended my case for the first six weeks of the experiment were these:—enormous irritability and excitement of the whole system: the stomach in particular restored to a full feeling of vitality and sensibility; but often in great pain: unceasing restlessness night and day: sleep—I scarcely knew what it was: three hours out of the twenty-four was the utmost I had, and that so agitated and shallow that I heard every sound that was near me: lower jaw constantly swelling: mouth ulcerated: and many other distressing symptoms that would be tedious to repeat; amongst which however I must mention one, because it had never failed to accompany any attempt to renounce opium —viz. violent sternutation: this now became exceedingly troublesome: sometimes lasting for two hours at once, and recurring at least twice or three times a day. I was not much surprised at this, on recollecting what I had somewhere heard or read, that the membrane which lines the nostrils is a prolongation of that which lines the stomach; whence, I believe, are explained the inflammatory appearances about the nostrils of dram-drinkers. The sudden restoration of its original sensibility to the stomach expressed itself, I suppose, in this way. It is remarkable also that, during the whole period of years through which I had taken opium, I had never once caught cold (as the phrase is), nor even the slightest cough. But now a violent cold attacked me, and a cough soon after. In an unfinished fragment of a letter begun about this time to —— I find these words: "You ask me to write the —— ——. Do you know Beaumont and Fletcher's play of Thierry and Theodoret? There you will see my case as to sleep: nor is it much of an exaggeration in other features.—I protest to you that I have a greater influx of thoughts in one hour at present than in a whole year under the reign of opium. It seems as though all the thoughts which had been frozen up for a decad of years by opium, had now, according to the old fable, been thawed at once—such a multitude stream in upon me from all quarters. Yet such is my impatience and hideous irritability—that, for one which I detain and write down, fifty escape me: in spite of my weariness from suffering and want of sleep, I cannot stand still or sit for two minutes together. 'I nunc, et versus tecum meditare canoros.'"

At this stage of my experiment I sent to a neighbouring surgeon, requesting that he would come over to see me. In the evening he came: and after briefly

stating the case to him, I asked this question:—Whether he did not think that
the opium might have acted as a stimulus to the digestive organs; and that the
present state of suffering in the stomach, which manifestly was the cause of the
inability to sleep, might arise from indigestion? His answer was—No: on the
contrary he thought that the suffering was caused by digestion itself—which
should naturally go on below the consciousness, but which from the unnatural
state of the stomach, vitiated by so long a use of opium, was become distinctly
perceptible. This opinion was plausible: and the unintermitting nature of the
suffering disposes me to think that it was true: for, if it had been any mere *irre-
gular* affection of the stomach, it should naturally have intermitted occasionally, and constantly fluctuated as to degree. The intention of nature, as mani-
fested in the healthy state, obviously is—to withdraw from our notice all the
vital motions, such as the circulation of the blood, the expansion and contrac-
tion of the lungs, the peristaltic action of the stomach, &c.; and opium, it seems,
is able in this, as in other instances, to counteract her purposes.—By the advice
of the surgeon I tried *bitters*: for a short time these greatly mitigated the feelings
under which I laboured: but about the forty-second day of the experiment the
symptoms already noticed began to retire, and new ones to arise of a different
and far more tormenting class: under these, but with a few intervals of remis-
sion, I have since continued to suffer. But I dismiss them undescribed for two
reasons: 1st, because the mind revolts from retracing circumstantially any sufferings from which it is removed by too short or by no interval: to do this with
minuteness enough to make the review of any use—would be indeed *"infandum
renovare dolorem,"* and possibly without a sufficient motive: for 2dly, I doubt
whether this latter state be any way referrible to opium—positively considered, or
even negatively; that is, whether it is to be numbered amongst the last evils from
the direct action of opium, or even amongst the earliest evils consequent upon a
want of opium in a system long deranged by its use. Certainly one part of the
symptoms might be accounted for from the time of year (August): for, though
the summer was not a hot one, yet in any case the sum of all the heat *funded* (if
one may say so) during the previous months, added to the existing heat of that
month, naturally renders August in its better half the hottest part of the year:
and it so happened that the excessive perspiration, which even at Christmas at-
tends any great reduction in the daily quantum of opium—and which in July
was so violent as to oblige me to use a bath five or six times a day, had about the
setting in of the hottest season wholly retired: on which account any bad effect
of the heat might be the more unmitigated. Another symptom, viz. what in my
ignorance I call internal rheumatism (sometimes affecting the shoulders, &c., but
more often appearing to be seated in the stomach), seemed again less probably attri-

butable to the opium or the want of opium than to the dampness of the house*
which I inhabit, which had about that time attained its maximum—July having
been, as usual, a month of incessant rain in our most rainy part of England.

Under these reasons for doubting whether opium had any connexion with the
latter stage of my bodily wretchedness—(except indeed as an occasional cause, as
having left the body weaker and more crazy, and thus predisposed to any mal-
influence whatever),—I willingly spare my reader all description of it: let it perish to him: and would that I could as easily say, let it perish to my own remembrances: that any future hours of tranquillity may not be disturbed by too vivid
an ideal of possible human misery!

So much for the sequel of my experiment: as to the former stage, in which
properly lies the experiment and its application to other cases, I must request
my reader not to forget the reasons for which I have recorded it: these were two:
1st, a belief that I might add some trifle to the history of opium as a medical
agent: in this I am aware that I have not at all fulfilled my own intentions, in
consequence of the torpor of mind—pain of body—and extreme disgust to the
subject which besieged me whilst writing that part of my paper; which part,
being immediately sent off to the press (distant about five degrees of latitude),
cannot be corrected or improved. But from this account, rambling as it may be,
it is evident that thus much of benefit may arise to the persons most interested
in such a history of opium—viz. to Opium-eaters in general—that it establishes,
for their consolation and encouragement, the fact that opium may be renounced;
and without greater sufferings than an ordinary resolution may support; and by
a pretty rapid course† of descent.

To communicate this result of my experiment—was my foremost purpose.
2dly, as a purpose collateral to this, I wished to explain how it had become
impossible for me to compose a Third Part in time to accompany this republi-
cation: for during the very time of this experiment, the proof sheets of this

* In saying this, I mean no disrespect to the individual house, as the reader will understand when
I tell him, that, with the exception of one or two
princely mansions, and some few inferior ones
that have been coated with Roman cement, I am
not acquainted with any house in this mountainous district which is wholly water-proof. The architecture of books, I flatter myself, is conducted
on just principles in this county: but for any other
architecture—it is in a barbarous state; and, what
is worse, in a retrograde state.

† On which last notice I would remark, that
mine was *too* rapid, and the suffering therefore
needlessly aggravated: or rather perhaps it was not

sufficiently continuous and equably graduated.
But, that the reader may judge for himself—and
above all that the Opium-eater, who is preparing
to retire from business, may have every sort of information before him, I subjoin my diary:—

First Week.				Drops of Laud.
Mond. June 24	.	.	.	. 130
— 25	.	.	.	. 140
— 26	.	.	.	. 130
— 27	.	.	.	. 80
— 28	.	.	.	. 80
— 29	.	.	.	. 80
— 30	.	.	.	. 80

75

reprint were sent to me from London: and such was my inability to expand or improve them, that I could not even bear to read them over with attention enough to notice the press errors, or to correct any verbal inaccuracies. These were my reasons for troubling my reader with any record, long or short, of experiments relating to so truly base a subject as my own body: and I am earnest with the reader that he will not forget them, or so far misapprehend me as to believe it possible that I would condescend to so rascally a subject for its own sake, or indeed for any less object than that of general benefit to others. Such an animal as the self-observing valetudinarian—I know there is: I have met him myself occasionally: and I know that he is the worst imaginable *heautontimoroumenos*; aggravating and sustaining, by calling into distinct consciousness, every symptom that would else perhaps—under a different direction given to the thoughts —become evanescent. But as to myself, so profound is my contempt for this undignified and selfish habit, that I could as little condescend to it as I could to spend my time in watching a poor servant girl—to whom at this moment I hear some lad or other making love at the back of my house. Is it for a Transcendental Philosopher to feel any curiosity on such an occasion? Or can I, whose life is worth only eight and a half years' purchase, be supposed to have leisure for such trivial employments?—However, to put this out of question, I shall say one thing, which will perhaps shock some readers: but I am sure it ought not to do

Second Week.				Drops of Laud.	Fourth Week.				Drops of Laud.
Mond. July 1	.	.	.	. 80	Mond. July 15	.	.	.	. 76
— 2	.	.	.	. 80	— 16	.	.	.	. 73½
— 3	.	.	.	. 90	— 17	.	.	.	. 73½
— 4	.	.	.	. 100	— 18	.	.	.	. 70
— 5	.	.	.	. 80	— 19	.	.	.	. 240
— 6	.	.	.	. 80	— 20	.	.	.	. 80
— 7	.	.	.	. 80	— 21	.	.	.	. 350
Third Week.					Fifth Week.				
Mond. July 8	.	.	.	. 300	Mond. July 22	.	.	.	. 60
— 9	.	.	.	. 50	— 23	.	.	.	. none
— 10					— 24	.	.	.	. none
— 11		Hiatus in MS.			— 25	.	.	.	. none
— 12					— 26	.	.	.	. 200
— 13					— 27	.	.	.	. none
— 14	.	.	.	. 79					

What mean these abrupt relapses, the reader will ask perhaps, to such numbers as 300—350, &c.? The *impulse* to these relapses was mere infirmity of purpose: the *motive*, where any motive blended with this impulse, was either the principle of *"reculer pour mieux sauter;"* (for under the torpor of a large dose, which lasted for a day or two, a less quantity satisfied the stomach—which, on awaking, found itself partly accustomed to this new ration): or else it was this principle—that of sufferings otherwise equal those will be borne best which meet with a mood of anger; now, whenever I ascended to any large dose, I was furiously incensed on the following day, and could then have borne any thing.

so, considering the motives on which I say it. No man, I suppose, employs much of his time on the phenomena of his own body without some regard for it; whereas the reader sees that, so far from looking upon mine with any complacency or regard, I hate it and make it the object of my bitter ridicule and contempt: and I should not be displeased to know that the last indignities which the law inflicts upon the bodies of the worst malefactors might hereafter fall upon it. And, in testification of my sincerity in saying this, I shall make the following offer. Like other men, I have particular fancies about the place of my burial: having lived chiefly in a mountainous region, I rather cleave to the conceit, that a grave in a green church-yard, amongst the ancient and solitary hills, will be a sublimer and more tranquil place of repose for a philosopher than any in the hideous Golgothas of London. Yet if the gentlemen of Surgeons' Hall think that any benefit can redound to their science from inspecting the appearances in the body of an Opium-eater, let them speak but a word, and I will take care that mine shall be legally secured to them—*i.e.* as soon as I have done with it myself. Let them not hesitate to express their wishes upon any scruples of false delicacy, and consideration for my feelings: I assure them they will do me too much honour by 'demonstrating' on such a crazy body as mine: and it will give me pleasure to anticipate this posthumous revenge and insult inflicted upon that which has caused me so much suffering in this life. Such bequests are not common: reversionary benefits contingent upon the death of the testator are indeed dangerous to announce in many cases: of this we have a remarkable instance in the habits of a Roman prince—who used, upon any notification made to him by rich persons, that they had left him a handsome estate in their wills, to express his entire satisfaction at such arrangements, and his gracious acceptance of those loyal legacies: but then, if the testators neglected to give him immediate possession of the property, if they traitorously "persisted in living" (*si vivere perseverarent*, as Suetonius expresses it), he was highly provoked, and took his measures accordingly. In those times, and from one of the worst of the Cæsars, we might expect such conduct: but I am sure that from English surgeons at this day I need look for no expressions of impatience, or of any other feelings, but such as are answerable to that pure love of science and all its interests, which induces me to make such an offer.

Sept. 30, 1822.